How to Find a Job in 6 Weeks

2nd Edition

Anthony Ranieri

How to Find a Job in 6 Weeks

2nd Edition

Copyright © 2003, 2012 Anthony Ranieri

First published in Melbourne in 2003 by Tandem Press

ISBN: 978-0-646-90252-4

DEDICATION

I dedicate this book to my two children, Anthea and Christian for the joy
they have given me and for making me so proud of them.

.

CONTENTS

ACKNOWLEDGMENTS

I want to thank the people of the Australian city of Ballarat for the memorable moments and support during the launch of the 1st edition of this book in 2004.

.

INTRODUCTION

Earlier in my career, I had the undistinguished task of laying off 250 workers due to an imminent plant closure. If you speak to any person in the human resources profession, they will tell you how mentally difficult it is to let people go and see their disappointment in the process.

Redundant employees express a wide range of emotion, ranging from family responsibility and financial insecurity to just losing a work-life they had grown to rely on and become accustomed to. It was my job to counsel employees about how they could better cope with their circumstances, and I hired professional workplace counsellors to assist.

What was to happen two weeks later was unprecedented. After a job well done and a smooth redundancy process, my managing director walked onto my office, thanked me for my efforts and made me redundant! 'I needed you to complete the process first before I could let you go,' he said. I felt as though I had hit a brick wall and was momentarily stunned. How was I to break the news to my wife? I had two young children; a mortgage like most of the working population and my wife did not work outside the home. This book is about how I coped with this stressful moment in my life.

I had to draw upon all my previous job-hunting experience

and survival skills to get through. I can break it down into five key critical success factors:

1. Successful job search skills knowledge
2. Strong financial management initiatives
3. Flexible and open career re-assessment
4. Mental toughness and a strong belief system
5. Managing your current job.

Successful Job Search Skills Knowledge
Key Success Factor Number 1

Your very first objective when you have lost your job is to get another job. Now that may sound a bit straightforward, but it isn't. To get another job today requires special knowledge and skill.

This is because, in most situations, redundancy falls during times of economic slowdown, rising unemployment resulting in fewer jobs and greater competition. Labour economists call this an 'oversupply of labour', and this will cause an imbalance in the labour market favouring employers. That's right – employers can pick and chose whomever they like, and they know it. I think that competition is a keyword here because just like any other competitive scenario, nobody remembers who came second.

The only winner is the person who gets that job, and you're up against it in what is the cruel market place. If you have been working in an organisation for a long time and are reaching the older age category, being out of work for the first time can shock you. All of a sudden, you're in a cauldron of job hunters operating in an unbalanced labour market where supply far outweighs demand.

Let's face it, it will not be easy, but there is always hope. Whatever you do, don't become defeatist and lose faith in your abilities. Get yourself in job search mode and learn all you can about job-hunting skills. It will be necessary for you to do this to compete at the same level and edge closer to winning that job.

Your job search knowledge must consist of the following areas of competence:

- Ability to tap into the hidden job market
- Good letter writing ability with a marketable resume
- Strong belief in yourself and mental stamina.

Successful job search skills knowledge is critical, and this book focuses heavily on this key area. I have covered all of the above areas of competence in separate chapters so that you can easily move from one key activity to another. Your ability to network with others and perform well at interviews will be paramount.

Your ability to write good covering letters and have a well-written up-to-date resume is equally important. If you need more coaching beyond the scope of the book, then go out and get it.

Strong Financial Management Initiatives
Key Success Factor Number 2

Money management is certainly an area of great stress during redundancy. This is because your comfort zone has been taken away from you. The weekly or fortnightly pay you have relied upon is no longer there, and you are concerned about where your next pay is coming from. I have seen this scenario cause great stress to people with debts, mortgages, and young families, particularly where there is only a single income earner.

I remember once a young man who was made redundant, and as Employee Relations Manager, I had to be the bearer of the bad news. He broke down and cried in front of me, not because he had lost his job, but because he had just bought a new house and had increased his mortgage. To make matters worse, his wife was expecting a second child, and she was not working. He was frightened to tell his wife and did not want to go home. I eventually spoke to his wife and decided to drive him home myself. The anxiety and pain he felt during this moment were tremendous.

I have always felt a correlation with money management and the ability to focus on getting a job. If you can take the pressure of monetary matters away from you for a short time, then your ability to focus on job hunting improves significantly. The distraction of money worries does not help you focus on interview performance and getting that job. You may become desperate and make the wrong career move in the name of security. You must focus on managing your money immediately after a job loss and here are ten financial tips to get you started:

1. Speak to your bank about lowering your mortgage repayments immediately. You will find that over the years you have probably increased your repayments either deliberately or through interest rate reductions. Pay the minimum amount possible for now and forget about paying your house off sooner. That is not a priority now, and you must review your financial objectives.

2. With your redundancy payment pay-off credit card debt either in part or full and decrease the number of bills and interest, you must pay monthly.

3. Eliminate all unnecessary spending. All those nice things to have, such as pay television, domestic servants, magazine subscriptions and memberships should be reviewed.

4. If you have money tied up in investments such as shares or fixed interest term deposits, withdraw this money either in part or full and create a buffer zone for emergencies. Hold this money every day 'at call' account for psychological security. This buffer zone will make you feel more secure and comfortable and allow you to focus on job hunting.

5. Watch your spending and don't behave as though you are still employed. This is the toughest part because it involves changing your lifestyle and habits. Holidays, clothes and any other regular purchases such as household items and entertainment expenses must be slashed. They are not important now, and you will survive until things are back on track again.

6. Be economical with controllable household utility expenses such as gas, electricity, telephone and your food budget. I

managed to save $150 a month on food for my family by just watching for price specials, comparing prices and being more selective.

7. Create a strict budget that is achievable and try to work within it. It will help you stick to targets and operate within set budget guidelines.

8. Apply for social security payments. The money will not be enough to live on, but it will stretch your savings further buying you more time for job search.

9. If your finances become too tight, prepare to refinance your home as a last resort. Again, this is not a preferred option, but the key to job success is time.

10. Talk about the prospects of borrowing money from family only if necessary. You will need a very supportive family for this and be prepared to pay them back when you get a job.

All the above tips are really common-sense applications, and I utilised them when I was unemployed. It helped me extract more time for my job search and relieved the pressure to focus on getting the right job.

I must stress that the key to financial management during redundancy is different and geared towards buying time to enhance your job search. I say this because you cannot pick and choose the timing of your next job offer. It could happen quickly or take longer than expected due to a range of factors, including a bit of bad luck. You must be mentally prepared for this and factor it into your financial management.

Flexible and Open Career Re-assessment
Key Success Factor Number 3

My advice in this instance gets out of your comfort zone whatever you do! Too many people I have helped in their career transition have hindered their job search prospects by sticking to old beliefs and methods of approach. It has to do with familiarity, and what people know best, a type of comfort zone holding you prisoner within an electric fence. Once you have lost your job, your life will change from despair to opportunity.

I say this because it's a perfect opportunity to try something new and different. That's right, you have nothing to lose now, and you can experiment and try new ideas and concepts. Stretch yourself and become excited with the thought that everything you have always dreamed of doing outside your steady and regular job has now arrived. It is time to try and test new ideas, experiment with new concepts or see where your hobbies will take you. I commenced writing this book to keep me busy when I lost my job.

Key success factor 3 is about open career re-assessment. To sit down and analyse your career options carefully rather than focusing on getting back to your regular day job or profession that you have been working for so many years.

It is time for a break and a re-assessment of your career wants and needs. In this book, I dedicate a chapter to career options. I recommended that you consider a variety of options, such as:

- Starting your own business or franchise
- Developing a new concept, idea or invention
- Consider going back to school and undertaking further studies
- Develop your hobbies into a potential income source
- Try a new career in a different industry and profession
- Take a sabbatical and enjoy the beautiful pleasures of the world.

Whatever you decide to do, flexibility in thought and total career re-assessment will enable you to increase your options in life. When you are in career transition mode, I can easily teach you job search skills and how to apply them; however, your view on life and how you exercise your career options is a thought process that only you can act upon. Life is all about increasing your options and then picking the best one for yourself.

Don't limit yourself when you lose your job, open yourself to all possibilities and explore your opportunities to their fullest. Would you believe I was motivated to write this book when I was between jobs? I had always wanted to write a book about assisting others in achieving better employment prospects, but I always thought it too hard and time-consuming.

The truth was that I had never written anything this substantial before and just the thought of commencing; it made me feel uncomfortable. I had some spare time up my sleeve, and I decided to give it a try, each day I wrote two or three pages, and my intensity and confidence grew each time. I also enjoyed it immensely and thought about writing as a new career. I reassessed my career options and was willing to try and experience other things, so can you!

Mental Toughness and a Strong Belief System
Key Success Factor Number 4

Losing your job is one of the toughest events that can happen to you in life. All of a sudden, your standard of living, prosperity and your perception of yourself is challenged. Not easy thoughts to deal with daily.

If you have a family with young children and a mortgage like the majority of us, then matters can get worse because others dear to you and reliant upon your steady employment are also affected. There is nothing like coming home to your partner and informing them you no longer have a suitable job and watching their jaw drop to the ground in a split second.

I learned very quickly that being sorry for myself was not going to help me, and what had happened in my previous job was over and done with. I could not change the past, but I could ensure that the present and future be better managed with a new way of thinking. The best way to get another job is to stay focused and challenged to be mentally tough. If you cannot do this for yourself, then do it for your loved ones who rely on you. Many authors describe this situation of downward spiralling anxiety and depression as 'learned helplessness'. You believe that no matter what you do, nothing can help you out of your current situation and that you are destined for doom and failure.

This is not true, learned helplessness will not get you another job, but mental toughness and a strong belief in yourself and your abilities will. All situations are temporary, and you are just entering a trough in your life cycle. Soon it will get better, and you will enter a resurgent growth stage and rise towards a new peak in your life.

However, you must believe in your abilities strongly because your belief system will control your thoughts and actions. A belief is nothing more than a feeling of certainty about what something means to you. In this book, we discuss belief systems in more detail and expose how you can better control your beliefs towards positive thinking. These are beliefs that can help provide you with energy and a form of mental toughness to keep you going in a positive direction.

Managing Your Current Job
Key Success Factor Number 5

I have made it very clear in my book that good jobs are hard to find today and that the oversupply of good candidates ensures that employers have the upper hand at recruitment. This is what we are dealing with in the new millennium, and sometimes we may lose sight of this and feel that the grass is greener on the other side.

Working as a professional employee relations practitioner for many years, I have seen many people leave good jobs simply because they were not good at managing or keeping their current employment. I don't mean that you should give up better opportunities, far from it. I am referring to those who have left their employment in difficult circumstances or were not entirely happy with their workplace circumstances at the time. It is easier for us to lose our composure rather than think about a situation through rationally during difficult circumstances.

The grass is not always greener on the other side. All businesses have their political issues, difficult people to get along with and peculiarities that don't always make sense, and perhaps, some companies are more prone to this than others. The key is to manage your career and your job better, whereas you can rationally think through those difficult moments and ensure you continue to maintain positive relationships in the workplace. All things pass in life, and sometimes it may be nothing more than a difficult phase the company is going through. If you are being counselled for poor performance, have a hard look at yourself and determine whether there is genuinely room for improvement.

You may find that you can turn it around with a dedicated personal approach and commitment. If someone is making your life miserable focus on better managing others in the workplace and see if you can change the situation by adopting new and different strategies to manage this person better. There are many courses, books and mentors in the workplace that can assist you to overcome difficult situations through their own experiences.

In this book, I talk about considering other career options. I want to reinforce a key point that the best time to do this is when you are employed. Develop other career paths and opportunities so that if your current job no longer provides you with the motivation and passion required, then you will be better prepared. It is really about your application to managing your job better that can make a difference in these circumstances.

I will review all the five critical success factors throughout this book; however, keeping in mind that job search skills knowledge is probably the most important of the five critical success factors. I had some advantage compared to others in the area of job search due to my human resources background. A lot of people would say to me, 'How do you manage to find jobs so quickly under the circumstances and end up with a good salary package?'

Having worked in human resources for many years and have recruited many employees for several organisations over this period has given me an insider's view of how the job-hunting process works. However, it is not just the system you apply to job hunting we are concerned about but your attitude to job-hunting that is very important.

I could teach you the most advanced job-hunting techniques available and interview skills necessary for successful job-hunting, however, if your belief system or application of these skills is not competent, then your chances of securing the right job in a short time frame will be diminished.

You will discover throughout my book that job-hunting success is directly related to the amount of time, energy and effort you put into it. It can be a very time-consuming, demanding and frustrating process.

It is my opinion that your ability to secure a better job, given all other socio-economic circumstances, should not take you more than approximately six weeks ideally. The longer the job-hunting process continues beyond this point, the more difficult it may become, and there are government statistics to show this later on in the book.

It also becomes difficult from a financial management point of view. Unless you are a member of the wealthy few, most of us eventually run out of money and the standard of living you become accustomed to may change dramatically.

Of course, achieving a job offer within a defined time frame will vary amongst professions, age group and educational background and is very dependent upon your circumstances and supply and demand in the market place. However, in the majority of cases, it is an achievable goal.

Job-hunting is predominantly about believing in yourself and your abilities. It is about portraying self-confidence and self-appraisal, constantly refining and developing yourself to a higher personal level.

Would you believe me if I told you that the majority of job candidates are assessed based on their fit to the organisation? Even though technical skills and experience are important, the overriding factor to job-hunting success is going to come down to your ability to interact with others. Your personality, values and perceived work ethics and how these important factors present themselves at the interview are a key measure for success. We are talking about a match between you and the employer that is predominantly based on whether you will fit the team and organisational culture.

I once had a frank discussion with a friend who was looking for a job for over nine months and could not secure a position.

I asked him why someone with his experience was taking so long to get a good job. He responded that all the jobs he had applied for and attended interviews were for some reason or another, not suitable.

After further discussion, it became apparent that his job-hunting philosophy was based on upon his views and interpretations of what companies should be looking for in a candidate.

He was trying to dictate the recruitment process himself, and this discouraged the employer. He also was not flexible in his approach. We discuss flexibility in salary packaging later on in this book. I suppose the body language and subtle message he was conveying to employers at interviews was that he was doing them a favour by just being present and that the job had to be on his terms.

If there is one bit of advice, I can give you right now, it is that employers don't necessarily care what you think of interviews because they already know what they want. Employers have spent years and a lot of money developing profiles of people that they believe fit their culture. If you don't appear to fit at the interview, then all the experience in the world will not get you the job.

The recruitment process, in most cases, is still heavily weighted in favour of employers, and they can dictate the terms as to how a candidate will be selected. Today, employers are also very careful in selecting candidates because of the cost involved in maintaining and training employees.

This is mainly due to increasing industrial laws and other regulations that can severely punish an organisation financially for any breaches. We are talking about unfair dismissal, equal opportunity and discrimination, health and safety and the involvement of trade unions, government departments, or other associations that monitor compliance of these laws.

A closer look at the employment market is always appropriate. We should all be aware of the labour market in which we are active. The point I am making is that job hunting is getting harder, particularly for better-paid and more sought-after jobs in good companies. I hope to provide you with enough information in this book to give you that extra edge, knowledge and advice by revealing the hidden secrets to job-hunting success based on my own experiences and successes.

1 TAPPING INTO THE HIDDEN JOB MARKET

Least Effective Job Search Techniques

Many job hunters engage in a job search without obtaining assistance from experts in the area. This results in having to resort to traditional job search techniques. How many times have you heard the comment, 'I think I had better start looking through the employment classifieds?'

Without being too critical, I must stress that this is a perfectly normal reaction. The key point is being aware that there are more productive and alternative methods you can apply to your job search. If you apply the job search techniques, I am about to demonstrate to you in this chapter; you will be more successful than you ever imagined in attaining the right job for you.

I also believe that given the correct circumstances, you should achieve your job search objective in less than six weeks and increase your total salary package by 10% as an outcome.

Recent government statistics on successful and unsuccessful job search experiences show that 21% of successful job seekers spent less than four weeks looking for work. This is the top quartile you need to aspire to be successful at job hunting. A closer look at the characteristics of these successful job hunters will be discussed later on in this chapter. If you believe that newspaper classifieds are a good place to focus your job search, then you are in fool's paradise. Most people commencing their job search normally resort to traditional methods because it is when their morale is highest, and to be frank about it, this is all they know or have been taught about looking for a job. It is our lack of job-search knowledge and awareness that usually places us at a disadvantage to others when we are competing for the best jobs. Be mindful though, that traditional job-hunting techniques are fine until the twentieth or so rejection and many months later without a job in sight. Job search is a time-consuming, demanding and sometimes stressful activity. It is not an activity you want to be performing for an extended period, and hence, it should be achieved within an intense and achievable time frame. You should avoid this trap of using outdated job search methods by following the simple and effective techniques presented in this chapter.

Sending resumes by the bucket load

Many misguided experts may advise you to target companies that interest you by forwarding your resume to the respective Human Resource Department. That's great in theory; however, everyone else who is looking for work is doing the same thing! Sending out resumes in their bucket load is one of the greatest fallacies of job-hunting.

The bottom line is that sending resumes in their bucket loads has a poor track record and companies today receive more resumes than they can manage. If you are lucky, you will receive a regret letter, and at worst, your resume will be filed with a pile of others never to been seen again.

If you believe this is a good use of your time, then think again. In the majority of circumstances, your resume will form the basis of ongoing paper shredding activity.

Many job hunters' resort to this strategy because it is less imposing. There is no personal contact involved, so rejection is hidden and easy to manage. We print out our resume and covering letter, place it in an envelope and post it to a prospective company. Psychologically we have fulfilled our job-hunting desire and minimised our self-consciousness knowing we have made a concerted effort in obtaining a new job. However, unknowingly, we have left the rest of the process to fate and the control of others. We are hiding behind an imaginary wall that is built on a lack of confidence and job-search knowledge.

An American study showed that there was only one job offer for every 1470 resumes received by employers. In most instances, if you are lucky, your resume will be screened in less than thirty seconds. Job-hunting is about increasing your odds and applying techniques that few job hunters are aware of or utilising. So, do yourself a great favour and forget about this technique altogether, it simply does not work!

Employment agencies – friend or foe

Most employment agencies only assist most marketable candidates. They are limited in resources and do not have the time to actively market you to employers if you are not a high-profile candidate. They focus on the best candidates, market them to employers with appropriate job vacancies and receive a good commission if they are placed. The average agency commission may vary between 8% for administrative positions and 15% for executive positions. Despite common perceptions, employment agencies do not have a database full of jobs. They may only be working on a few assignments at a time. If an employment agency has pursued your application with employers and you have been unsuccessful on a few occasions, it is unlikely they will assist you further. If you are in career change mode and unemployed, it is unlikely they will market you again.

This is because it is too hard, and the turnover required, based on time and resources applied, does not make it a feasible proposition. It is all about making money, and employment agencies know perfectly well where their bread and butter come from. Again, the question of who is in control of the job search process is brought to your attention.

I have known individuals who have approached job search by putting too much faith into two or three employment agencies, expecting them to take on board the responsibility for securing those individuals a job.

You should consider that the average employment agency placement rate is only 5%. This is not a good hit rate, in my opinion.

So, the message here is to use agencies strategically as part of a broader job search strategy and not to rely on their support in full. Later in this book, I discuss using employment agencies more strategically to your advantage.

Responding to newspaper advertisements

This is probably the most traditional method for job hunting used by people. Instinctively it is the first-place job hunters look for job opportunities. The disappointing part of this approach is that you have limited yourself to approximately only 25% of the available job market. That is, 75% of jobs are not advertised in the mainstream media. So, you are not getting is not the full picture as far as the labour market is concerned.

We resort to this form of job-hunting because it does not involve people contact, and the fear of rejection is minimised. This gives a sense of security to those generally lacking job search skills and who feel that job hunting can be achieved without the adoption of other more creative techniques. The problem is that the majority of other job hunters feel the same.

Therefore, most job hunters are applying for a limited number of good jobs that are advertised in newspapers. If you look at basic economic rules and the laws of supply and demand, then it is obvious that the demand for good jobs will outstrip supply if you apply this job search technique only.

You have increased your levels of competition and decreased your chances of success dramatically. It is not a good common sense when you place yourself at a disadvantage.

Answering newspaper ads will not lead to a job for 75% of job seekers who try it. Within 48 – 96 hours after an advertisement appears in the newspaper classifieds the employer or recruiter will receive between 50 – 200 resumes depending on the type of job advertised. Approximately 90 – 95% of resumes will be screened immediately, leaving a shortlist of between 5 – 10 candidates, depending on the calibre of the applicants. The recruiter will probably spend around 30 seconds on your covering letter and possibly your resume if you are fortunate enough.

These are not great odds if you are relying only on this method for securing employment. Responding to newspaper advertisements should be part of a much broader job search strategy and not relied upon as the only media for seeking job opportunities.

Seeking government employment services

The Australian Federal Government has contracted to private providers the responsibility of providing employment services to the community that previously was managed by the Centrelink.

The Job Network comprises a national network of providers that are a community, government and private organisations dedicated to finding employment for unemployed people and particularly the long-term employed. Employment service providers are agencies that provide various kinds of support for people looking for work. There are many providers across Australia, delivering different kinds of assistance.

The truth of the matter is that Employment Service Providers are limited in the assistance; it can provide certain classes of unemployed persons. These private providers working under the Job Network banner are compensated for every person or case they manage into securing employment. It is very much an incentive system, so the greater the number of employment placements, the greater the monetary reward.

For more info on Employment Service Providers go to the following web site:

www.jobsearch.gov.au/

If you are from a professional background, it is unlikely that private providers will find you suitable employment. The reason is employers do not use their services for recruiting professionals or highly skilled personnel. It appears that the majority of cases managed by Job Network providers are focused mainly on long-term unemployed, unskilled to semi-skilled positions or difficult to manage cases.

For professionals, the probability of finding work through such private providers is approximately 13%, and if employment were obtained, it would most likely be of a part-time or temporary nature. If you are from a professional background, it may pay to consider other job search techniques.

However, if you belong to the category of unskilled workers, require retraining or are a school leaver looking for your first job, services offered by private employment providers may assist you. They will also assist you if you are looking for part-time or casual employment. Private providers are also good at managing difficult cases such as people with disabilities, long-term unemployed or people undergoing rehabilitation for work-related injuries.

The Network Approach

Networking is the tool that binds the non-traditional job-hunting approaches previously mentioned. Your ability to network effectively will provide you with a gateway to the hidden job market.

Remember that the hidden job market represents 75% of jobs that are not advertised. The network approach is a pro-active method that is useful to all job hunters irrespective of their professional background. It will be your key driver in tapping into 75% of jobs that are not advertised.

One key attribute or trait I have found amongst several successful job hunters is their networking ability. They spend a lot of time communicating and making new contacts all the time. They are constantly out there building new relationships with key people. I know this does not come naturally for some of you. However, it is not expected that you become the best networker in the world but at least become proficient at it. It will be tough at first; however, with persistence, you will develop this technique and succeed at it. The following exercises will help you establish techniques for developing your network that you thought did not exist. It is amazing how many people I have encountered who did not realise how wide or extensive their network was.

How many people do you know?

You will be surprised at how many people the average person knows. It's estimated that the average person has approximately 100 contacts. The following table will assist you in identifying people you know. Commence with writing their names now! It's always best to create two lists; one for people you know personally and the other for business contacts.

Below is a table with possible networking contacts to get you started.

Personal	Business
Family members	Professional contacts
Personal friends	Customers
Doctor	Trade associations
Accountant	Personnel agencies
Dentist	Business owners
Bank Manager	Suppliers
Religious associates	Contractors
Sporting contacts	Networking groups
Members of Parliament	

ACTIVITY ONE

By identifying ten personal and business contacts, you will be able to commence setting up the network meeting as described on the next page.

Identify and write ten personal contacts into the fields below:

1.
2.
3.
4.
5.
6.
7.
8.
9.
10.

Identify and write ten business contacts into the fields below:

1.
2.
3.
4.
5.
6.
7.
8.
9.
10.

Setting up the networking meeting

Networking is probably the most effective tool for tapping into the hidden job market. Networking is about using your current circle of friends and contacts to establish a greater network. The greater your network, the better your odds of achieving your job success.

Networking moves job hunting to a more personal level, where relationships and connections are important. Think about this for a moment, if you were a manager of a business wouldn't you prefer to hire someone referred to you by someone you know or trust.

It makes perfect sense because you are decreasing your chances of recruiting the wrong person. The person you know or trust has a vested interest in referring the right person to you because they understand your needs better than strangers.

Setting up the networking meeting for the first time will require some effort on your behalf. This is because self-marketing does not come naturally to some of us. Job search is about marketing your transferable skills to potential employers. Those who are good at marketing themselves to employers get jobs first. I remember when I made my first phone call, and it was not easy.

It took a lot of courage and will power; however, I was determined to make a start. I contacted someone easier to start with that I had a professional relationship through an employer association. It was amazing how genuinely helpful he was and prepared to assist me in whichever way possible.

One thing I learned about this process is that after a couple of calls, your confidence grows and it is remarkable how many people want to help you when you are asking for assistance. To ease the pain, I recommend initially, and you contact those people you know best. The list of ten personal and business contacts you noted in activity one, represent those you know best. Start with those contacts by following the basic techniques outlined below.

Your goals

• When calling your contact by phone ask for a twenty-minute meeting—The- objective is to provide your contact with a copy of your resume and to seek their opinion on your skills and industries you may be suited
• Discuss industry matters at the meeting such as business trends, career prospects and current issues
• Ask for a referral so that your network of contacts will expand
• Do not ask for a job or infer that you are looking for a job specifically in your contact's company.

Your telephone techniques

Use phrases in your telephone introduction as follows:

• I am sure you can help me
• I am in job search mode
• I would appreciate it if you would look at my resume and make referrals to others in appropriate industries.

Do not do the following:

• Don't read your introduction from a script
• Don't ask for a job, you must project yourself as seeking information
• Be clear and concise and sound confident

- Don't commence the conversation on the defensive, 'I'm sorry to bother you'
- Don't refer to the word interview; use personal meeting instead.

Setting up the networking meeting in advanced stages

By this stage, you should have developed some experience in contacting people you know well, however, how about those people you don't know so well that have been referred to you by your initial network contacts? Your goals and objectives in this instance are the same as on the previous page.

Just because you are now required to contact people you don't know so well, does not mean changing our basic techniques. You have developed some experience by now, and you should be capable of answering more inquisitive questions from network contacts. My advice is to be sharper and more accurate in your responses during discussions with your new network contacts. Here are some points to consider that will help you along the way:

- Don't focus on your reasons for leaving your current or previous job; it only detracts from your objectives
- If your contact recommends you send your resume in the mail, try to avoid this by focusing on a personal meeting instead—Your resume will only end up in the recycling bin
- Your telephone introduction must focus on projecting an industry move and gathering information in a much stronger way than with your previous contacts
- Ring your network contact before 8:45 am and after 5:00 pm to avoid being scrutinised by the secretary
- Prepare a short paragraph or bullet point list summarising your work history and career objective.

Additional tips

- Aspire to at least two personal meetings per week
- Keep a running log to document your meetings and phone calls to contacts and the outcomes of those meetings
- Accept as many referrals as possible from your network contacts during network meetings
- If you must speak to the secretary during your initial telephone call to your network contact, give the impression that you know your network contact from a previous association
- Don't ask or refer to possible vacancies; you will destroy the integrity of this process for everyone else who tries it. You must project a need for help and information only
- If your network contact is not present or is unavailable at the time you call, ask what time you can call back. If the secretary wishes to acknowledge the purpose of your call, inform the secretary you are researching industry trends and career prospects within the industry.

ACTIVITY TWO

Select two personal or business contacts and call them to arrange a personal meeting.

Document your meeting on this page.

Meeting One
Contact Name:
Company Name:
Meeting Summary:
Referral 1:
Referral 2:

The network meeting

After all the hard work of getting yourself through the door and into the office of your network contact, you will need to follow some basic principles to ensure maximum benefit and protocol from your meeting as follows:

- Reinforce to the network contact that you are there to obtain information, not a job. You are marketing and not selling yourself
- Avoid talking about your reasons for leaving your current or previous job
- While your network contact is reading your resume, expand on your key strengths and transferable skills
- Leave your resume with your network contact after the meeting
- Remember to ask for a referral to expand your network
- Write a follow-up letter to thank your network contact for their time—This will be explained to you on the next page
- Ensure the meeting does not turn into an interview. If your network contact commences interviewing you, reinforce that you are there to gather information only. Your contact may then elaborate whether they have a position in mind and that interview type questions are necessary to evaluate you for that position
- Your follow-up letter should be handwritten and project a personal statement
- Ensure you research the company you are visiting and prepare a list of questions accordingly
- Follow-up with your network contacts in one month to advise them of your progress and the usefulness of their referrals. You will be surprised how many people take an interest in your progress.

Targeting companies

Networking can be taken one step further by identifying companies you wish to work for. It requires that you list your transferable skills and then develop a list of companies that are most likely to use those skills. Once you have identified such companies, you should direct your network meetings in that direction. This is a great way to prioritise your network meetings.

Check with your network contacts if they know people within your preferred list of companies and use the same basic principles to set-up a meeting with your referral.

ACTIVITY THREE

Sample Follow-up Letter

Write a follow-up letter to one of your network contacts that you have held a personal meeting.

Private and Confidential

Dear Julie

Thank you for your time in meeting with me today. I found you to be dynamic and in tune with your business. Your comments on industry trends and issues were very stimulating.

The information and advice you provided me were very helpful in expanding my knowledge of the industry. Thank you for your referral and recommendation to contact Michael Brown for additional information. I plan to contact him this week, and I will be pleased to inform you how my meeting went.

Please keep my details and objectives in mind should you come across any suitable vacancies. As we discussed, I will contact you in one month to keep you informed on my progress.

Yours sincerely
John Candidate

Getting jobs in faraway places

We are an international community. People today are willing to move to other countries to obtain new skills and experiences. This may be in the form of a working holiday, temporary or permanent employment. Some of the reasons people are willing to work in other countries are:

- Lifestyle and climate
- Better job opportunities
- Obtain greater international experience
- Target specific industries
- Increased remuneration and other benefits
- Returning to home town.

Techniques for finding work in other countries

Networking principles may be difficult to follow when seeking work in other countries due to distance and practicality. Here are some techniques that may assist you in finding work in other countries:

- Obtain a copy of the local job classifieds from the country you intend working in and familiarise yourself with the job market in that country
- Write to the local chamber of commerce of the country you intend working in and seek further information on the industry you wish to be employed
- Write a list of contacts you have in the country you intend working in

• Use the Internet to learn more about the political climate of the country you wish to work in and also access relevant and most predominant job web sites.

The networking letter

• Ensure your letter of introduction is written in a personal manner and refers to a mutual friend in your introduction
• Send your letter approximately two weeks before visiting the country you intend working in
• If you don't have a contact or mutual friend to refer to in your letter, then make use of an article or project the company you are targeting is involved in
• The body of the letter should be in bullet point form highlighting your key strengths and abilities
• You may refer to a key project or achievement that stands out within your industry as part of your introduction
• Don't send your resume – however, make a concluding statement that your resume is available upon request
• Your letter should be no longer that one page.

Additional tips

• The Internet is a great way to source job classifieds in other countries and to obtain a feel for the local job market
• The Internet may also assist in obtaining connections in other countries by visiting local job sites and newsgroups
• Familiarise yourself with working Visa requirements for the country you intend working in.

SAMPLE INTRODUCTION LETTER

Private and Confidential

Dear Julie

With your knowledge of the .... area and the automotive industry, I believe you might be able to help me with answers to some questions I have in connection with a planned relocation to the area. I'm writing in the hope that you'll be willing to grant me a few minutes in this regard.

Since .... I have served in the engineering division of Dynamic Automotive Pty Ltd with responsibilities ranging from Engineer, Project Manager and Manager, R&D to my current position of Manager, Engineer and R&D. Amongst other things; my work has involved the following areas.

List in bullet points several subjects of likely interests from your background

*
*
*

I will be in .... for the week commencing (date), and would very much appreciate the opportunity of meeting with you to get some advice and direction as to what activity in .... is relevant to my background. I would also welcome the opportunity to share ideas of mutual professional interest.

I will call you in several days to arrange a mutually convenient appointment. I look forward to meeting with you.

Yours sincerely
John Candidate

Advice on working in Australia

If you are from outside Australia and are curious about working possibilities in Australia temporarily, then the following types of entry requirements or categories will be of interest to you.

I have made references back to the Australian Department of Immigration web pages should you require further information. Australia has strict rules of entry, and it is recommended that if you desire to have a longer stay, then you should seek advice from the regional Australian Embassy to determine your obligations.

Working holidaymaker visa

The *working holiday maker visa* gives you twelve months to travel to Australia from the date the visa is granted. You can travel in and out of Australia any number of times within those twelve months.

The main purpose of a Working Holiday Maker Visa is holiday and travel. Any work should be incidental to supplementary funds, that is, periods of work should be broken up by periods of holiday and travel. You may work full-time, part-time or casually, for three months at a time with any one employer. You are not permitted to extend your employment beyond three months with any one employer.

The *working holidaymaker program* aims to promote international understanding. It provides opportunities for resourceful, self-reliant and adaptable young people to holiday in Australia and to supplement their funds through incidental employment.

Australia has reciprocal working holiday arrangements with the United Kingdom, Canada, Japan, Ireland, the Netherlands, the Republic of Korea, Malta and Germany. These arrangements allow for young person's 18 – 30 years of age to holiday for up to twelve months in Australia, with the opportunity to supplement their funds through incidental work.

Only applicants from working holiday arrangement countries who are aged between 18 and 30 years old, single or married, and have no dependent children are eligible to apply for a Working Holiday Visa. To be granted a Working Holiday Visa applicant also have to show that:

- Their main reason for coming to Australia is to holiday (any work carried out should be incidental to supplement funds)
- They will not undertake studies or training for more than three months; and
- They will leave Australia at the end of their authorised stay.

The Working Holiday visa cannot be granted in Australia. All Visa applications must be made overseas. Citizens of the United Kingdom, Ireland, Canada and the Netherlands can apply at any Australian mission overseas. Citizens of Japan, Malta, Germany and the Republic of Korea must apply in their own country.

Information on the location of the Australian Department of Immigration and Multicultural Affairs overseas is available on the Internet by visiting:

www.homeaffairs.gov.au

For further information on the Working Holiday Maker Visa, visit the above web page;

Temporary residence entry

The temporary residence category includes a temporary entry for stays of up to four years in a wide range of categories. The most substantial of which are students, skilled employees, people are establishing businesses and working holidaymakers, with smaller numbers in categories such as sportspeople, media and film staff, entertainers, religious workers, retirees and occupational trainees.

The *temporary residence program* also allows Australian employers to recruit staff (usually with particular skills) from overseas. For detailed information on these categories, please see the Sponsoring Temporary Overseas Employees booklet at:

www.homeaffairs.gov.au

Please be aware that temporary residents are required to pay taxes on income earned in Australia. They do not have access to social welfare benefits or national public health cover. Citizens of countries with which Australia has Reciprocal Health Care Agreements are entitled to emergency medical insurance cover. This cover does not extend to pre-existing conditions. Applications must be lodged at an Australian overseas mission, not within Australia. For a full list of overseas missions visit:

www.homeaffairs.gov.au

Visiting Australia on business

Below are the categories for entry into Australia for business purposes:

- APEC Card
- Streamlined entry for APEC member countries

- Business (Short Stay) For visits of up to three months
- Business (Long Stay)
- Temporary residence for up to four years
- International Events and Conferences
- For those organising international events.

Looking for jobs on the Internet

Using email to access jobs

Email can be used effectively to access jobs on the Internet, whether it be newsgroups, uploading your resume to job sites or making contact with employers directly. Unlike sending unsolicited resumes, you will find that most professionals read their emails and are more likely to read your message and take note of your resume details. However, pay attention to email protocols and do not abuse this.

The power of newsgroups

There are many newsgroups or discussion groups that relate specifically to job hunting. There are so many that they are sub-divided into categories such as resumes, jobs, job classifieds, specific occupations and much more. Posting your resume to newsgroups, responding to jobs advertised or following a lead is all part of accessing Internet jobs. The following are Australian newsgroups for your consideration:

aus.ads.jobs
aus.ads.jobs.resumes
au.jobs

The strength of ezines

Subscribing to specialised career and job search Internet newsletters or ezines, as they are commonly known, can help you develop your job search skills and knowledge while also providing you with leads to vacancies that have not been advertised. Ezines are free and contain plenty of useful career information, leads and links to job sites and resources you did not know about.

Receiving jobs by email

Isn't technology great! Now you can have jobs sent to your email address according to criteria that you have requested. Many job sites that specialise in job advertising have this facility. These sites collate jobs from a wide range of resources and then list them in their database for distribution to subscribers for free. Australian job sites worth vising that have this facility are:

www.seek.com.au

www.jobnet.com.au

https://au.indeed.com

www.careerone.com.au

How to format your files

If you plan to send your resume to newsgroups, job sites or contacts by email, it's important to remember that not everybody has Microsoft Word, and many people share different versions of Word. To avoid this problem, I have always recommended sending your file attachment by email in text format. This way, there are no problems for the receiver. Creating a text file is simple.

1. Open your document in Word
2. Click on the file and save as
3. Change save as type to text only
4. Give your file a new name and enter save

Now you can use this file containing your resume specifically to attach to your email.

Which is the job site for you?

Job sites vary according to their philosophy and business objective. Some job sites have a greater emphasis on providing advertised jobs, while others focus on careers knowledge or resume distribution. Whatever their specialisation, you may feel more comfortable with a particular site for various reasons.

My thoughts are that some job sites are too big and have become less personal in their service. This is a problem because most job seekers need as much support and help as possible. My advice is to try as many jobs sites as possible and get to know their strengths and weaknesses before deciding which is the one for you.

How can employers find you online?

Many job sites offer a matching service, whereas employers looking for candidates may perform a search for job seekers with required skills. My advice is to visit job sites and to use this free service. It may require that you post your resume in a text format as discussed above or that you enter your details into an online form.

Employers can also find you online when they visit newsgroups. Employers are always on the lookout for experienced staff, and they use newsgroups to search for potential applicants. Visit the list of Australian newsgroups previously mentioned.

2 LETTER WRITING SKILLS AND RESUME PREPARATION

Effective Letter Writing

Your covering letter or letter of application is the first of three documents used during the job search process.

1. Cover Letter
2. Resume
3. Follow-up Letter.

Many applicants underestimate the power of a well-written covering letter, assuming the recruiter will only focus their attention on the resume. In today's working environment, a recruiter's workload has increased dramatically by having to complete a higher number of recruiting assignments and screening an increasing number of applicants.

The bottom line is that the recruiter is a very busy person, under constant pressure to complete assignments within a shortened time frame. This is where the power of a well-written covering letter affects. It is the first document a recruiter will read, and it is here that you must sell yourself and convince the recruiter to look further into your resume. You must convince the recruiter that your resume is worth their valuable time to read. It is your statement, an invitation to look further.

In this book, I have limited the sample resumes, and letters to those that I believe are effective through my experience. Overloading you with sample resumes and letters will only confuse you and detract from expressing your personality and personal style.

Your resume and covering letter must reflect your individuality and your personality. I will provide two examples of a resume and a covering letter format that I feel have worked well for me and others I have coached through this process.

The covering letter has been tried and tested with excellent results, so when you are on to a good thing, you may as well use it to its fullest potential rather than re-invent the wheel. Have a look at the layout and structure of the covering letter and add your style and personality when putting it together.

How to structure a covering letter

- Ensure your achievements and accountabilities address the key selection criteria
- Your letter should not exceed one page
- Keep your letter simple and ensure your paragraphs and sentences are short and concise
- Use bullet points to highlight key achievements and accountabilities
- Avoid using negative phrases
- Don't over-sell yourself; reflect balanced thinking
- Review and re-draft your letter until you are confident with it

- Check for spelling mistakes and ensure it is correctly addressed
- Use good quality stationery and prepare your letter on a computer word package
- Ensure it is printed on a good quality printer
- Your introduction should be your strongest selling point, referring to your greatest achievement
- Ask for a personal meeting as opposed to an interview as your concluding statement.

Letter writing tips

- Don't use coloured stationery; it may give the impression you are over-selling
- Address the letter to the person responsible for the recruiting assignment. • If the job advertisement does not state their name, ring and find out
- Your strongest selling points must reflect the key selection criteria
- Don't mention you are unemployed or have been made redundant. It may reduce your chances of being interviewed
- Don't state the obvious when writing your letter:

E.g. please find my resume enclosed or I am applying for the position of…

Do not attach your photo unless requested.

SAMPLE COVERING LETTER

Private and Confidential

Dear Julie

Re: Human Resources Officer

I have ten years' broad experience in human resources with the last five years being in an employee relation's role, predominantly in the manufacturing and retail industries.

My accomplishments and abilities include the following:

- *Developed and implemented a national personnel policy and procedure manual*
- *Managed the occupational health and safety function nationally*
- *Providing service and advice on day-to-day employee relations, policy and procedures to employees and line management*
- *Developed and implemented a Federal Agreement and prepared a draft Head Office Administrative Employees Agreement*
- *Experience in targeted recruitment and selection techniques*
- *Experience in HR systems including Excel and Word*
- *I hold a Bachelor of Business in Personnel and Industrial Relations.*

I also wish to highlight my skills in assessing training needs and developing in-house competency-based training.

My personal qualities consist of working as an effective team member and as an internal consultant. I work well under pressure, possess good organisational skills, and can work on many projects simultaneously.

I look forward to the opportunity to meet personally.

Yours sincerely
John Candidate

Writing a follow-up letter

A follow-up letter is a powerful tool often ignored by applicants during a job search. Written effectively, it can add weight to your application, particularly when a shortlist for second or third interviews is being determined by the recruiter. The follow-up letter has several uses:

• A method for continued dialogue between yourself and the recruiter
• An opportunity to restate your skills and experience
• Evidence that you have considered the position seriously and wish to reaffirm your interest
• It is a proactive document, providing a vehicle for selling yourself further
• The ability to offer solutions to key issues and objectives discussed during the interview.

How to structure your follow-up letter

The structure for your follow-up letter is similar to your covering letter with some minor variation as follows.

• Commence your letter with a thank-you statement in appreciation of the recruiter's time
• Include references to key selection criteria discussed during the interview in bullet-point form. This will confirm that you have paid attention to the recruiter's comments
• Be proactive by offering solutions to key issues and objectives discussed during the interview

- Reaffirm that you are still interested and challenged by the position. It will reflect your enthusiasm.

Follow-up letter tips

- Write your letter on the same day as the interview
- Send your follow-up letter on the same day as the interview. It is important that your
- The letter gets to the recruiter as quickly as possible
- Fax or e-mail is an ideal method of correspondence; otherwise, send it express post.
- Normal mail is too slow
- Do not courier your letter, as it may appear exaggerated. Write a follow-up letter after each interview stage and not just the first.

SAMPLE FOLLOW-UP LETTER

Private and Confidential

Dear Julie

Thank you for the time you took for our meeting today in providing me with an understanding of the role and responsibilities of the Human Resources Officer position. I found you to be dynamic and in tune with the needs of the business. Since you plan to reach a decision fairly quickly on a shortlist, I feel it would be useful to comment on several specific needs we discussed and my abilities for meeting them.

• You indicated recruitment needs to be centralised and coordinated, respectively. I am confident that my previous recruitment experience in manufacturing will provide me with the skills to review and develop new systems in this area

• My experience in the delivery and development of competency-based training modules will be relevant to the central coordination of training and identifying training needs within the organisation

• My experience in managing the occupational health and safety function has provided me with a solid background in this area. I see the potential to add value through continuous improvement to this important function

• My specialised strength in employee relations will be of value when dealing in day-to-day industrial issues and in renegotiating your Enterprise Agreement in future.

I wish to reinforce my service philosophy and my belief in working as part of a close team.

Once again, thanks for your time. I look forward to hearing from you shortly.

Yours sincerely
John Candidate

Forwarding correspondence

Many job-hunters forward job applications not realising what takes place on the other side. This lack of awareness is a major reason why many applications do not get past first base.

The recruiter is a busy person with several recruiting assignments to coordinate at any given time. They must deal with an endless number of phone calls and perform other duties as part of their broader accountabilities. You can increase your chances of having your application read by following some basic principles.

• Forward your covering letter and resume only. Do not include any other attachments; if they are required you will be asked at the interview

• Your resume should be no longer than two or three pages. If it is longer, you are limiting your chances of having it read by the recruiter

• Use standard A4 paper and avoid using strong colours. If you must use colour ensure it is very subtle

• Do not bind your resume or use fancy packaging techniques; it will only add to the pile and frustrate the recruiter

• Faxing or emailing your covering letter and resume is a good alternative to mail. It is quick, efficient, and requires less handling by the recruiter

• If mailing your application, ensure that the envelope is addressed correctly.

Correspondence tips

• Remember! Don't add to the recruiter's pile; ensure your job application is no longer than three pages including your covering letter
• Send your job application by mail in an A4 envelope; don't fold it into a standard letter-sized envelope.

Documenting correspondence

As with many job hunters, the probability is that you will apply for more than one advertised position. It is therefore essential that you keep a separate running sheet for each position you have applied for, noting the outcomes during each stage of the process.

Record keeping for job applications will assist you in:

• Recalling the details of the recruiter for future correspondence
• Identifying extended periods during stages of the interview process for follow-up
• Organising and controlling the job application process in a systematic and disciplined manner.

Writing a winning resume

To improve your chances of job search success, you must increase the ratio of job interviews per application. The greater the number of interviews you can attend, the greater your chances of securing a job. This is why your resume is so critical in the process.

A professionally written resume that can capture the eye of the recruiter will go a long way towards helping you achieve this objective. I have worked on an interview per application ratio of about 30%. That means I hope to secure at least one interview for every three targeted job applications I send-off.

This ratio will fluctuate between individuals and is dependent upon a range of factors such as individual experience, the industry sector, health of the economy and time of year to mention just a few. You should keep tabs on your interview per job application ratio as a measure of your job tracking. Just divide the number of interviews by the number of job applications and then multiply by 100.

I do not intend this as the *100 different ways to write a resume* book. I feel sure that you have seen many books dedicated to nothing but resumes. What I fail to understand is how these books can assist you. A resume is a very personal document about you and your skills, strengths, qualifications and achievements.

You are providing a potential employer with an introductory insight into you. It is your entry point and should be viewed as a marketing tool rather than just a text description of your employment history, skills and qualifications. As with any marketing tool, it is about selling yourself (the product) most attractively, and to do that, you need an understanding of what drives employers today. That's right; you are a product selling goods and services that happen to be your skills, experience, qualifications and achievements. A good resume will contain all of these qualities in a concise document.

Today we are fighting for the time and attention of the employer, and they do not have much time for you to impress them. Your resume, if you are lucky, will be given little time to impress the recruiter. If your resume is sent unsolicited, it will only be read at a glance, 20 – 30 seconds maximum if you are fortunate.

The point I wish to make is your resume has to grab the intention of the reader quickly and effectively. Presentation and format can be important; however, language and the words chosen can also have an influence psychologically on the reader. Employers want and need people who are solutions-oriented and can solve key company problems within their respective functions. If your resume does not demonstrate this, it will be left on the scrap heap.

A book full of resume templates with all the right words and descriptions can never depict you as an individual. There are some finer points about writing a resume that has assisted me in my job search experience that I want to share with you.

If you can take note of these points and translate them into a template provided, then it will most likely work for you. If you have a family friend who can read your resume and make a comment, then that will be useful. Ask your friends to comment on how your resume communicates your strengths, skills, personality, and achievements and whether it is a genuine representation of you. If you prefer that a professional prepare your resume, then be sure to choose someone with the right background and qualifications in this area.

Many people are claiming to be experts in resume preparation, and all they are doing is transposing information on to a fancy resume software program. It may look good on paper, but it may miss the most important ingredient, which is about representing you as a person. Many of these resume preparation services are run by people with no knowledge of job search or the recruitment process. Unless they can make this connection with companies and their recruitment needs, then what translates onto paper can be very ineffective.

There are two styles of resumes; chronological and functional. I prefer to use a chronological resume because it is easier for the recruiter to follow. I find that functional resumes may be good in highlighting your key skills or functions. However, recruiters tend to get somewhat lost in them and seem to gravitate to a chronological representation during the interview anyway comfortably.

Here are some finer points to assist you in preparing your resume.

A Chronological resume has four main sections:

1. Personal details
2. Career objective
3. Career history
4. Personal qualifications.

• Type your resume on a word processor or computer and print clearly on plain white paper
• Ensure your resume is no longer than two or three pages and with no attachments
• Ensure there are no spelling mistakes
• Only use original copies when applying for jobs
Ensure your resume is up to date and accurate
• Do not bind your resume or place it in a folder or file, staple it and attach it to your covering letter.

Remove unnecessary information, such as:

• Marital Status
• Sex
• Age
• Salary

- References
- Nationality
- Place of Birth.

Include a career objective at the beginning of your resume

- It should be no more than fifty words and a statement of your career aspirations
- Ensure your career objectives state the major skills you possess and how these skills can add value to an organisation.

List your employers in chronological order commencing with the most current

- List at least 3 – 6 key achievements and skills with each employer
- State examples of your achievements in current or previous companies

Employers are interested in problems that you can solve for them.

List your qualifications and memberships to professional bodies

- State your educational qualifications
- List any relevant internal courses you completed
- List your memberships to any professional associations.

References

- References should be provided upon request and not stapled to your resume

- If an employer is interested in your references, then that will be communicated at some stage of the interview process
- Most employers wish to make contact with relevant employers, preferably your most recent boss or other influential managers you have interacted with during recently held positions.

A Functional Resume Sample

- Name
- Address
- Telephone numbers
- e-mail address

List key traits

- Industrial relations strategist
- Strong leadership qualities
- Champion of people

Career overview & capabilities
Summary of key achievements or key skills and knowledge areas as shown by examples below:

- Highly developed industrial relations expertise and proven sharp negotiation skills in dealing with unions and other institutions and government authorities
- Extensive human resources management experience in tough manufacturing environments and services sector
- Competency-based training knowledge and experience in implementing training systems at the workplace level
- Experienced in managing others and providing key human resources and business advice to senior and executive managers
- A champion of people by fostering closer and better cross-cultural workplace relations.

Key achievements
List major area of expertise as shown by example below:

- Negotiated a distribution centre enterprise agreement for a division of blue-chip Australian company with the National Union of Workers covering all warehouse employees on site
- Provided industrial relation support and advice to senior managers across a multi-site business structure for a division of a blue-chip Australian company
- Successfully introduced Australian Workplace Agreements to select warehouse and manufacturing employees to obtain key flexible working arrangements
- Developed strategy for Australian workplace agreement implementation
- Negotiated Australian workplace agreements with individual employees and representatives
- Managed legal process, document wording and lodgment to relevant government authority
- Managed business downsizing and redundancy program eventually leading to business closure for a large automotive components manufacturer and successfully negotiated redundancy conditions with union
- A key member of the strategic committee on business strategy for downsizing, union negotiation and site rationalisation planning
- Instrumental in driving strategic negotiations with the relevant union on redundancy conditions after the announcement, and negotiating a successful outcome by a strategic business plan

• Developed programs and strategies for better co-operation, harmony and workplace relations between management, employees and their unions.

Training and development

• Lodged successful tenders for $50,000 in training funding to deliver a broad range of industry-specific competency-based programs at the workplace
• Formulated and implemented a comprehensive strategic competency-based training model for a division of a large blue-chip Australian company
• Performed task analyses and skills audit to identify training needs
• Introduced a new internal training framework consisting of standard operating procedures, coaching plans, assessors guide and handbooks
• Linked the training model to a competency-based performance pay structure for skilled factory employees
• Introduced and implemented the front-line management program for supervisory and middle-level managers across various sites
• Managed the application process and developed the training infrastructure to obtain Registered Training Organisation status
• Developed an in-house skill tracking and competency-based software management tool that is now available commercially.

Human resource management

• Managed a department of up to 5 diverse human resource professionals and several key contract and facilities providers
• Contributed to financial year budget cost-down process by reducing the human resources budget by up to 10%

• Developed human resources department strategic direction by linking key initiatives to corporate business plan

• Experienced in performance management systems for annual appraisal process and salary review for management and staff employees.

Career progression

Position 1

Company

Location

Dates

Place a summary of the principal function of your role (2-3 sentences). Bullet point of key achievements and key knowledge areas, as shown below:

• Established industrial relations objectives for enterprise agreements with relevant unions and developed ongoing productivity improvements

• Ensured a healthy and safe work environment through the implementation of safety policy practices and procedures

• Implemented a comprehensive training plan for plant operators and developed cross-skilling throughout the business and to ultimately improve production output and quality

• Managed all industrial negotiations and workplace relations on-site with operational management, relevant union organisers and shop stewards

• Established and reviewed all human resources and safety policy and procedures to ensure compliance with legal requirements and company standards
• Managed performance appraisal systems and annual salary review processes
• Knowledgeable in safety map and ISO auditing procedures and business requirements for compliance.

Position 2
Company
Location
Dates

Place a summary here of the principal function of your role (2-3 short sentences).
Bullet points of key achievements and key knowledge areas:

• Was 1 of the 2-person team that redrafted the company's Distribution Centre Employee Agreement
• Redesigned all company employee relations, occupational health and safety, and workers' compensation procedures to reflect current legislation and societal expectations on a national basis
• Initiated the use of OH&S performance indicators as criteria for store manager performance appraisals.

Education and affiliations
List educational details and affiliations, as shown below:

Bachelor of Business, Phillip Institute of Technology, 1990
Majors in personnel and industrial relations

Workplace Trainer Category 2 (Certificate IV), Casey TAFE, 1998

Associate Fellow Australian Human Resources Institute

Member, Australian Institute of Training & Development

Referees

All referees can be provided on request

A Chronological Resume Sample

Name
Address
Telephone numbers
e-mail address

Career objective
To use my technical, management, and interpersonal skills to add value to a private or public organisation by improving the work practices and procedures with which its employees are managed.

Career history
Employee Relations Manager
1 April 2001 – Current
Company here
Appointed to this position on an ongoing contractual basis to manage the employee relations function and to develop strategies for the implementation of an occupational health and safety system, review current enterprise agreement arrangement in various states and to develop a competency-based training system nationally for car detailers.

Major achievements:
• Successfully negotiated Federal enterprise agreements nationally at major airport locations and key regional centres with employees and relevant union
• Preparing applications for registration of agreement to the AIRC and representing the company on a range of industrial matters

- Developed and implemented an industrial relations strategy for Western Australian staff based on new industrial laws in that state
- Developed and implemented an occupational health and safety system comprising of policies and procedures, standard operating procedures, training and generic tools to manage OH&S at the operational level
- Developed and implemented a competency-based training system for car detailers nationally, consisting of standard operating procedures; training plans and assessment plan together with TAFE as a key partner
- Managed and reviewed the current performance management system by introducing new tools and appraisal format for greater effective staff measurement and alignment to key competencies and organisation core behaviours.

Human Resources Manager
1 Jun 2000 - 23 Mar 2001
Company here

Appointed to this position on a 12-month contract basis to manage the human resource function and to negotiate an enterprise agreement for manufacturing-based employees during campaign 2000 and to effectively downsize the business leading to the eventual closure.

Major achievements:
- Successfully negotiated an enterprise agreement during campaign 2000 with key productivity off-sets
- Negotiated on behalf of the company with the militant metals division of the AMWU

• Developed and implemented a strategy for negotiation during the enterprise agreement process

• Achieved approximately $200,000 productivity savings by negotiating and implementing three key productivity items

• Managed business downsizing and redundancy program eventually leading to business closure for a large and successfully negotiated redundancy conditions with union

• A key member of the strategic committee on business strategy for downsizing, union negotiation and site rationalisation planning

• Instrumental in driving strategic negotiations with the relevant union on redundancy conditions after the announcement, and negotiating a successful outcome by a strategic business plan

• Achieved re-accreditation for SafetMap Victoria after extensive preparation, assessment and internal auditing of OH&S policy, procedures, systems and work practices

• Formulated and implemented a comprehensive strategic competency-based training system for metals operators consistent with national training competencies and developed new classification and wages structure to assist in promoting new career paths.

Senior Human Resources Officer
19 Jun 1998 – 22 May 2000
Company here
Appointed to this position on a 6-month contract basis to implement a comprehensive training plan while providing a wide range of human resource services to line managers and textile manufacturing based employees.

Major achievements:

• Introduced a comprehensive training plan for manufacturing-based employees consisting

• Selection of training coordinators to deliver training on-site and their accreditation as workplace trainer category one trainers and assessors

• Performed task analyses and skills audits and identified training needs

• Introduced a new training framework consisting of standard operating procedures, trainers and assessors guides and handbooks

• Introduced a traineeship program in coordination with the training plan

• Maintained industrial harmony within manufacturing operations

• Recruitment of manufacturing-based employees and professional staff

• Performance counselling of manufacturing-based employees and staff

• Maintained human resource statistics and developed new statistical reporting processes.

Employee Relations Officer
23 June 1997- 12 June 1998
Company here

Appointed to this position on a 12-month contract to implement workplace reform at a chemical manufacturing site by introducing workplace change programs in consultation with the Australian Workers Union (AWU).

Major achievements:
- Introduced a comprehensive training plan for operators on site
- Selection of training coordinators to deliver training on-site and their accreditation as workplace trainer category two trainers
- Performed a task analysis and skills audit and identified a training gap
- Introduced new training procedures, processes and structure
- Introduced multi-skilling elements into the training plan
- Established industrial relations objectives for the basis of the next site enterprise agreement with Australian Workers Union as they relate to ongoing productivity improvements and workplace reform
- Introduced a health and safety induction program for contractors in CD format which included the measurement of competency
- Performed internal audits as required under ISO 9000
- Managed all industrial negotiations on-site with AWU shop steward and organisers.

Human Resources Consultant
Company here
1996 – 1997

Appointed to this position on a *9-month* contract to provide generalist human resource services and advice to key client groups. Major responsibilities include performance management, job evaluations, recruitment, counselling, employee relations and project work.

National Employee Relations Officer
Company here
1992 – 1995

Appointed to this position to develop policies and provide strategic advice in human resource practices and procedures to operating regions nationally for this major Australian retailer, with initial responsibilities for policy setting at the national level.

Major achievements:
Produced, and was 1 of the 2 -person team that implemented, a new Federal Award for store-based administrative and sales staff (70% of total staffing), that:

- The ordinarily extended span of working hours by over 30%
- Reduced casual loadings by up to 40%
- Reduced overtime penalty payments by 40%
- Reduced late-night trading penalties to zero
- Established common terms and conditions of employment throughout   Australia
- Established single union representation within all stores
- Provided reducing dependence on casual staff, from 7% in the first year
- Constituted major workplace and cultural reform in the organisation.
- Reduced casual loadings by 40%.
- Was 1 of the 2-person team that redrafted the company's Distribution Centre Employee Agreement
- Redesigned all company employee relations, occupational health and safety, and Workers' compensation procedures to reflect current legislation and societal expectations
- Initiated the use of OH&S performance indicators as criteria for sore manager performance appraisals

•Negotiated with the WorkCover Authority to achieve workers' compensation rebates for successful OH&S practices
• Was 1 of the 2-person team that established the company as a self-insurer for workers' compensation in its largest Australian operating region

Professional qualifications and affiliations

Bachelor of Business, Phillip Institute of Technology, 1990 *(Majors in personnel and industrial relations)*
Associate Fellow, Australian Human Resources Institute
Workplace Trainer Category 2.

Writing a Winning Resume

Power words to apply to resumes

Below are a few words to get you started that can be used to commence a phrase when describing your achievements in your resume. They are words employers like because they reflect leadership qualities and solutions-based initiatives. Try to think of other words that may reflect your achievements to use in your resume.

Negotiated	Instrumental	Represented
Developed	Initiated	Designed
Achieved	Introduced	Coordinated
Managed	Contributed	Influenced
Successfully	Ensured	Coordinated

Power phrases to apply to your resume

Below are some phrases I have used in my resume that can be applied to your resume to reflect key achievements. Achievements are important because they reflect what you are capable of professionally, and they also demonstrate your potential. Achievements need to be true and credible, so don't just use everyday achievements. Focus on milestones, projects and your key initiatives that have brought about a benefit or change to the company. Power phrases can be used to describe achievements where you have:

- Reduced costs of a specific process.
- I have completed a major project on time.
- Lead a team of others in achieving a major goal.
- Introduced a personal initiative or implemented an idea.

Below are some examples of power phrases I have used to demonstrate my achievements:

• Managed business downsizing and redundancy program, eventually leading to business closure for a large automotive components manufacturer and successfully negotiated redundancy conditions with the union.

• I have formulated and implemented a comprehensive strategic competency-based training model for a division of a large blue-chip Australian company.

• I have managed a department of up to five diverse human resource professionals and several key contract and facilities providers.

• I have contributed to financial year budget cost-down process by reducing the HR budget by 10%.

• I have lodged successful tenders for $50,000 in training funding to deliver a broad range of industry-specific competency-based programs at the workplace.

• Achieved approximately $200,000 productivity savings by negotiating and implementing three key productivity items resulting from enterprise bargaining negotiations.

.

3 INTERVIEW AND PRESENTATION SKILLS

The Meaning of Communication

If there is one key point or critical activity that distinguishes all the skills necessary for job-hunting success, it is communication. Your ability to communicate effectively with the interviewer and to read the style, intent and direction the interviewer is leading the interview is critical. You can be technically brilliant in answering all the questions at an interview; however, if there is no mutual attraction or fit, then your chances of job success may be reduced substantially.

Communication at interviews is about being able to express yourself clearly, answer questions appropriately and sending a clear message as to your style and personality. You want to be yourself at an interview and not someone else. An experienced interviewer will sense this. You must express your individuality so that the interviewer can assess more accurately whether you are a fit for that particular work environment or not. You want that fit also so that you can also feel secure in knowing that you will get along with others in that work environment as a team.

With many positions advertised today, there is an abundance of people contesting that one job and most of them have a good technical background for the position. So, what distinguishes the winner from the rest of the pack is communication. Your ability to capture the imagination of the interviewer and quickly establish a relationship with them is paramount.

A positive attitude backed by confidence and an ability to express your views exceptionally well is also a key skill. In a way, it is a sales and marketing exercise, except for the product you are selling, are you? So imagine yourself as a consumer brand and that you are attempting to sell the benefits to the buyer who in this case, is the employer. Remember that the employer is buying your services, intellectual capital knowledge and expertise as a total package.

Communication can be described as consisting of three main parts:

- Words
- Tonality
- Body language.

When you communicate with others, you perceive their response and react with your thoughts and feelings. Your ongoing behaviour is generated by your internal response as to what you see and hear.

Understanding that we communicate in more ways than just words is advantageous during the interview process. Interviewers will not only listen to the quality and content of your verbal response but also make assessments based on your tonality and body language. It is important during the interview process that you maintain rapport with the interviewer by using words, tonality and body language. Words are only a small part of the way we communicate with others.

Research shows that:

- Your body language determines 55% of communication
- 38% is determined by the tone of your voice
- 7% is determined by the words that you choose.

Interview Styles Recruiters Like to Use

The interview methods which human resource professionals prefer to use and the application of recruitment company standards, policies and procedures drive the recruitment process. Recruitment techniques are also driven by the latest trends in recruitment theory and practice. Like fashion, it will spread to companies like the latest seasonal launch in clothing. That is why learning a generic technique for answering interview questions will assist you in the majority of interviews.

Most recruiters pride themselves on using the latest recruitment techniques. So as a job seeker, learn about the latest trends in recruitment techniques. I will provide you with the latest recruitment techniques used by recruiters today so that you may better prepare for the interview process.

The panel interview

Many companies prefer the panel interview because it allows for assessment by more than one person. Normally the human resource professional and a line or operational manager will be involved in the recruitment process. Sometimes you may find more than two company representatives on an interview panel, particularly with government departments that have recruitment policies stating a certain number of department representatives by gender must be present.

You will most likely attend more panel interviews than a one to one interview. The panel interview can be more difficult to manage for the job seeker. This is because you are interacting with more than one person at any given time. You will need to master the panel interview if you are to be successful in your job search. Companies prefer the panel interview for the following reasons:

- Risk of choosing the wrong candidate is minimised
- The line manager or supervisor is involved in the process
- It is timely, requiring fewer stages in the recruitment process
- It can determine how an applicant performs in a more interactive setting
- There is a consensus decision-making process applied during selection.

Stress interview

Recruiters only use the stress interview if it is purposeful. This is because many candidates do not respond well to it. In my experience, even the best performers at interviews stumble at the stress interview. The purpose of any interview is to learn as much as possible about the candidate by creating a relaxed atmosphere.

Sadly, this is where the stress interview falters by putting you under pressure during the interview process. It is unlikely you will encounter this style of the interview unless you have applied for a position that requires high levels of pressure, stress and mental toughness. This style of the interview may be used by the armed forces, police and similar institutions as a deliberate attempt to measure your composure and reaction to intense and pressure situations. This interview technique is not used frequently by recruiters and is not in vogue. It is unlikely you will be subjected to this form of the interview unless the interviewer is very inexperienced and not trained properly in recruitment techniques.

Behavioural interview

By adopting a behavioural style of interviewing, companies are seeking to find out what makes you tick by digging into your past experiences and behaviour. The interviewer will ask you situational type questions by requesting you refer to past work experiences.

The rationale for this technique is that past work experiences are a good indicator of future performances. It is also a good way of confirming your achievements and skills as listed in your resume. The beauty of behavioural questions is that interviewers seem to have swapped the questions around between them, and there are a consistent number of generic behavioural type questions they will ask you. Some smarter interviewers will try to change the question around to confuse you. However, they are fundamentally seeking a similar response.

Without wishing to sound as though I am cheating but rather taking advantage of weaknesses within the current system of behavioural interviewing. It is just like filling out your tax returns within the scope of the law but maximising your return. I found a way of beating this interview-style by memorising past and relevant work experiences that could be applied in response to a select number of generic behavioural questions.

It takes a lot of practice on your own to get to a standard where you can draw upon your reserve of answers at interviews. Many of these pre-arranged answers can be applied to a variety of similar behavioural questions. So the first thing to do is to become acquainted with a list of generic behavioural questions soon to follow.

More about behavioural event interviewing (BEI)

I was lucky to work with one of the most prolific organisational psychologists in Australia, who was an expert and a leading authority in the technique of Behavioural Event Interviewing. I was grateful to have experienced being interviewed by him for a job. By the way, I got the job and went on to learn more about this fascinating interview technique.

Behavioural Event Interviewing (BEI) can be defined as:

An interview technique based on the premise that the best predictor of future behaviour is past behaviour.

- It allows the interviewer to:
- Gain detailed job-related examples
- Assess past performance
- Assess competences
- Confirm achievements noted in the resume.

The purpose of (BEI) is to best match the candidate's skills, competencies, and motives with the requirement and the success factors of the position. Well, you are probably saying, 'isn't that normal of interviewing anyway?'

Professor David McClelland, the creator of (BEI) believed that commonly used IQ and personality tests were poor predictors of a candidate's competency. He argued that companies should hire on competency in relevant fields.

A good example of this is if you are hiring a Cost Accountant. You should apply the competencies relevant to that field when interviewing. In the past, you would have been required to sit a generic IQ test, personality test and then respond to some very generic questions at the interview. Professor McClelland's once-radical ideas have become standard instruments in many corporations today.

A better explanation of competency can be defined as:

The skills, areas of knowledge, attitudes, and abilities that distinguish high performers.

These are characteristics that may not be easily observed at interviews but exist 'under the surface'. A good way for interviewers to flush out these competencies is by using behavioural questions. Competency can be made up of the following parts:

• Knowledge
• Skills
• Traits
• Motives.

All these parts make up what is observable behaviour. The benefits to the interviewer are as follows:

• Provides objective criteria for assessing candidates
• Allows interviewers to collect specific details about candidates work and educational experiences
• Focuses the candidate to provide more than 'canned' responses

The benefits for the candidate are just as good:

• Provides a chance to talk in detail about work and school experiences

- Offers opportunity to highlight strengths
- Provides a chance to reveal work styles and priorities.

So, there you have it. If you want to succeed at interviews, then become familiar with (BEI). My experience is that the majority of companies use this interview technique either in full or part. There are many derivations of this style, and they are defined in many ways. However, the basis for the interview questions is much the same. That is that the best predictor of future behaviour is past behaviour.

Preparing for a behavioural Interview (BEI)

One of the benefits of behavioural event interviews for the candidate is that it can be managed better than other interview techniques. Instead of being subjected to trick rather meaningless questions, you can prepare your dialogue and responses to questions.

A great place to start is to ensure that you are in tune with your resume and the accomplishments and achievements you included. Questions will be asked of you requesting detailed accounts of specific events from your work experiences. Generally, these questions begin with a phrase as follows:

Give me an example of the last time you...'
Describe your toughest situation where you...'

You must be very specific in your answers, and you must stick to the facts, it is just like telling a good story.

The interviewer will probe with follow-up questions that focus on:

The situation (what specifically happened)

- What was the project?
- What were the circumstances?
- When did it happen?
- What brought this problem to your attention?
- What made the situation difficult?

What you did or said

- Tell me exactly what you did?
- What did you do next?
- What steps did you take in handling the situation?
- What caused you to be so successful in this particular situation?

Some examples of behavioural type questions that I have collated over some time following. These common behavioural questions can be used to find specific answers that focus on the **situation** and your **involvement** as I have done for you in the example below.

Describe a time when you worked on a team that was having difficulties?'

I spent a semester working with a project team for my psychology class...
Our assignment was...
My responsibility was...
We had difficulty because...
My reaction/thought process was...
The results were...'

Key behavioural interview questions to master

It may be advisable to print or copy these pages so that you may note down your responses at some point.

Write down your responses to the following questions. It will help your thought processes in establishing pre-determined responses and to get you thinking and practising this interview style.

Innovativeness

Can you think of a change, which others would recognise as resulting principally from an idea or innovation you developed and implemented?

Question Response

Describe the situation:

What were your actions?
What was the result?

Persuasiveness

Describe your most satisfying or disappointing experience in attempting to gain management support for an idea or proposal you put forward.

Question Response

Describe the situation:

How did you persuade?

What was the result?

Judgment

Describe the last time you made a difficult decision and how you managed that situation.

Question Response

Describe the situation:

What was the decision?

What was the result?

Negotiation

Describe to me a situation where you were required to negotiate an important outcome and whether you achieved your aim.

Question Response

Describe your role as negotiator:

How did you negotiate?

What was the result?

Building Rapport

What cues do you look for in trying to establish relationships with groups or individuals? Provide me with an example when you used these cues to achieve a specific goal or outcome.

Question Response

Describe the situation:

What were your actions?

What was the result?

Tolerance for Stress

Describe a pressure situation you have been under in recent years. How did you cope with it?

Question Response

Describe the situation:
How did you cope?

What was the effect?

Have you ever been present when someone has lost their temper at work or became irritable? Describe it to me.

Question Response

Describe the situation:

What were your actions?

What was the result?

Self-Organisation

When scheduling your time, how do you determine what constitutes a top priority? Give examples.

Question Response

Describe the priority:

How you determined priority:

What was the result?

Teamwork and Co-operation

Describe a situation in which you wished you had acted differently with someone in your workgroup.

Question Response

Describe the situation:

What were your actions?
What was the result?

Individual Leadership

Give an example of where you have led others in solving a problem.

Question Response

Describe the problem:

What were your actions?

What was the result?

Career Ambition

How does this position relate to your short-term and longer-term career goals?

Question Response

Describe your career goals:

Some Answers to behavioural questions I have answered

Can you recall a time where you were able to utilise an informal network to influence critical people to support and accept a particular policy or procedure? How did you know that utilising an informal influencing process would be most effective in achieving your objective?

Answer: The proposed introduction of computer usage and Internet usage policy is certainly a good example of a policy that managers were skeptical about in the first instance. Many traditional-style, operational managers probably did not understand what the fuss was all about! The downloading or viewing of offensive and pornographic material is certainly a societal value that the company wanted to project as inappropriate. There was a strong view by myself that the business had to drive the correct behaviours, and in particular as far as EEO policy was concerned. There are several factors when trying to influence the behaviours of others that one must be familiar with:

• To have greater self-awareness of the views of others on a particular issue

• To ensure that by education and training a greater understanding will be developed by others

- To gain the support of key directors, general managers and even the managing director.

Developing relationships with key managers is a necessity for any HR Manager. It allows the manager to have a more informal relationship where views can be shared in a more open environment.

Sometimes this will not happen the first time, and however, with persistence, most people will come to share your view on key issues and respect your opinion as a professional. This type of lobbying or networking approach to business assisted me in getting the support of key managers in this instance. More importantly, to understand why the company wanted to introduce this policy.

This way, when a policy is issued, it has already received the informal understanding and support of most managers and is more likely to succeed and be used effectively.

Discuss a particular project you have led, where it was necessary to keep several teams informed and motivated over an extended period. How did you keep the project on track while maintaining your level of self-motivation?

Answer: The introduction of a competency-based training system for manufacturing-based employees is a great example of a team effort that required constant motivation over eighteen months. As with most manufacturing managers, their number one focus is not always training and development, and there are pressing manufacturing issues that are priorities first.

This did not help my cause as far as keeping the project on time and schedule. It was only my persistence that ensured this project did not go off the rails. One technique was coming up with solutions to manufacturing problems that training and development could address.

So, I made training look like an important tool they could use to their benefit. The introduction of competency-based training provided opportunities to multi-skill staff and offers a greater degree of flexibility for manufacturing managers. Once this was demonstrated, time and time again, it became obvious that training had an important part to play in their business.

The key point here is that HR did not own training and that I delivered ownership to the line managers. They became accountable for the implementation of competency-based training within their environment. I adopted a coaching or mentor-type role to ensure the levels of technical expertise were available to them. I was the leader of the training team that was responsible for this project.

We met regularly to discuss training developments and to draw upon one another's expertise to seek solutions. The training team was a cross-functional team containing members of the manufacturing division and ancillary services. The team was empowered to make decisions on most day-to-day issues and some strategic issues that would be escalated to the directors for decision-making.

I have always been personally motivated to achieve outcomes and solutions for the business. These are my strengths. The greatest satisfaction comes from being able to assist others in achieving their ultimate goals and objectives.

Discuss an instance where you have utilised your ability to read into a situation to detect potential, yet an unspoken problem. How did you utilise your initiative feel to prevent the issue escalating further?

Answer: During *Campaign 2008* enterprise bargaining negotiations with the union, our discussions with the union were reaching a stage was the impasse had to be broken. Our company was not the first auto components manufacturer to settle with the union, and this satisfied the MD.

However, as the HR Manager, I was receiving inside information from various sources. Information from contractors, supervisors and even organisations we engaged in a business that indicated that the union was gearing up for prolonged industrial action and that it could happen within a few days.

I also had received notice of a mass meeting of union members to be held in two days to discuss what action could be taken against the company. This was a potential problem that was not openly discussed or spoken about by management at the time.

The company was unprepared, with inadequate stock reserves in some key components and was unable to withstand a dispute extending beyond seven days. This would have had an impact on production shortly after.

I advised the General Manager and the MD of the situation and the requirement for a decision to either prepare for escalation of the negotiations or to commence settling the matter with the union and get whatever was salvageable from the process. After a key and important management team meeting, it was decided that the company would concede to the union demands and remove any threat of possible strike action.

I was always aware of our management attitude to strike action and the loss of face if we could not honour our requirement to supply without disruption. It was inevitable that the company would concede under these circumstances, as fighting on for a better outcome would have certainly meant a prolonged industrial disputation.

Detail an example where you have persisted with a particularly difficult plan until the objective has been achieved. What obstacles did you encounter in the process, and how did you overcome them?

Answer: In December 2005, my General Manager advised me of impending plant closure to take effect on June 2001. This was advised to him by our parent company. I was then asked to join a strategic management team to commence making arrangements for the closure with other senior managers.

This proved very difficult because it meant managing a human resource department in 'maintenance mode' without giving away through our day-to-day decisions that there would be severe downsizing of the business. This was also made more difficult by already strong rumours throughout the business that the company was gearing towards a plant closure shortly. This proved a tremendous obstacle.

My role changed from change agent to one of just keeping the peace with the unions and employees. My objectives were to stick to the ultimate plan or goal of closing the plant with minimal disruption to production in the interim period. So basically, maintain harmony and good relations with the union and our employees. This proved difficult at times; where I was required to concede on issues with the union that normally I would not have compromised on.

We eventually reached our goal and announced the closure without leakage of any information to those outside the strategic team, even though rumours continued in growing intensity during the period of planning. Our goal of plant closure was achieved without major disruption.

I achieved my goal by ensuring strict confidentiality and managing the human resource functions as though it was business as usual and being creative enough to ensure there were no longer-term decisions made beyond the proposed closure date. By consulting with others on the strategic team of any impending issues that threatened to divulge the closure plan.

Making active attempts to influence events to achieve goals; self-starting rather than accepting passively; taking action to achieve goals beyond what is required; being pro-active.

Answer: I recommended a project to introduce a balanced scorecard to aid and better manage strategic direction in manufacturing. I found many of the company's project initiatives to be quite loose and uncoordinated and lacking direction.

I hired a leader in this area to present to the management team the benefits of a balanced scorecard approach. The company was pleased with this strategy and commenced making arrangements to implement it.

This involved visiting other companies that had already progressed down this path with some good results. This was a pro-active approach in terms of addressing some issues in the workplace at the strategic level. The goal was to achieve a more coordinated approach to strategic management.

It assisted in better coordination of projects such as autonomous teams, statistical process control, classification structure and renegotiation of the enterprise agreement.

Being new to the company, it required a lot of effort in influencing others behind the scenes, particularly in selling the benefits of this approach and how it was helping solve real manufacturing issues.

Tips on answering behavioural type questions

• Refer to achievement in your resume when answering behavioural type questions
• If your response refers to a major project you were part of, break it down into smaller phases clearly and concisely when responding
• Be specific about your role in each situation
• Don't talk to fill up dead air. Take a minute to collect your thoughts and organise your answer before replying
• Use statistics or other measures in your response to back up the information you have provided
• Always turn a negative situation into a positive
• Always reflect on your ability to work as part of a team and to look for solutions to problems
• Show examples where you have done more than expected
• Prepare your responses to common behavioural questions before attending the interview
• Explain what you learned from each experience
• Demonstrate how you solved a specific organisational problem
• Remember, that you are telling a short story of a specific situation from the beginning to the end, and it is not uncommon for a good answer to take up to 5 – 10 minutes
• Ask the interviewer if they would like more detail.

20 key questions to master

It is unfair to provide you with an encyclopedia of interview questions and expect you to become proficient in their use without overloading you with information. This is not productive, particularly when our objective is to get you to adapt to interviewers and a range of interview questions.

It is unlikely that memorising answers to 100 interview questions will get you through the interview process. At interviews, you must be able to think clearly and adapt and modify your responses quickly rather than respond verbatim.

The following sample questions will assist you in answering a range of generic interview questions that are not necessarily behaviour based. This list is not meant to be exhaustive, and you will likely encounter questions not mentioned in this book. The point is that authors of books that detail every question conceivable are doing you a disservice. I am more concerned about your ability to think on your feet, to expect the unexpected, and then to be able to answer that question to the best of your ability.

I know this is easier said than done because it requires composure, confidence, a rational thought process and experience of interviews. However, this can be managed with practice and interview experience. Seek to attend as many interviews as possible to practice your responses and to learn from them each time. You will find that you will grow in confidence with each occasion and become more adaptable at interviews. Practice with friends and family if possible. Further on in this book, there are some exercises to help you through this objective.

What have you been criticised for in the past four years?

Reply: Provide an answer that is not so serious or trivial that it will disqualify you.

'I offered some ideas I thought were constructive but was told not to rock the boat.'

Did you agree or disagree with the criticism and why?

Reply: Agreeing with some of the criticism is a better response than agreeing with none of it at all.

Where would you like to be in five years?

Reply: 'I'd like to be at your job.'

How do you expect to get there?

Reply: Be clear and specific as to how you will meet the requirements and responsibilities to your career plan. Avoid common answers like 'hard work' and 'attending courses'.

What would you like to change in this job to make it ideal?

Reply: 'I don't think it should be changed, I do think it has to be mastered, and that is a challenging and exciting opportunity.'

How would you describe the most or least ideal boss you worked for?

Reply: 'I can adapt to any style, particularly to someone who can give me enough directions, so I have a specific idea of what's expected from me and then enough restraint not to hover over me every step of the way.'

What activities in your position do you enjoy most?

Reply: This question is designed to reveal your dislikes. The interviewer will refer to the opposite of your answer when describing the activities, you enjoy most. The best way to answer this question is to think about how the activities you enjoy most can reveal your dislikes. You can do this by simply applying the opposite to your answer. For example, the opposite of 'being part of a team' is 'bad morale'.

How would you describe yourself in three adjectives?
Reply: Combine your answer to convey strengths in both ability and personality such as determined, likable, and successful.

How would your subordinates and peers describe you with three adjectives?
Reply: Answer the same as for question 8 and smile.

What would you do if you detected a peer falsifying expense record?
Reply: 'Report it'.

What would you do if the company you had just joined gave you $3,000 to spend during the first year in any way you felt appropriate?
Reply: 'A job-related use.'

If you had a choice, would you rather draw plans or implement them?
Reply: 'Draw plans, not implement them.'

State three situations in which you did not succeed and why?
Reply: Admit to having failed at something. One example is too few,

and three is too many. Stick to two examples.

When you fire someone for a reason other than retrenchment, what would be your key reason for doing so?
Reply: 'That I felt I was acting in the best interests of both the company and the individual concerned'.
Why? Reply: 'From the company's point of view, the employee's performance did not meet our standards and expectations.'

What needs do you expect to satisfy by accepting this position?
Reply: Track the company's needs very closely. 'By achieving satisfaction by setting new goals and objectives and achieving them.'
We all fib occasionally; would you say something that is not entirely true? Give me three examples when you did.
Reply: 'I don't think everybody lies. I have known people who have never lied, so I don't think your premise is correct. When I have lied, I have kept it to social situations.'

What benefits can you expect from threatening an employee to do better?
Reply: 'Threatening employees is not an attempt to improve performance. It is a calculated prelude to dismissal. The hope is the employee will get the message and move on before being dismissed.'

If you encounter serious difficulties on the job, what would they be?
Reply: You are concerned about success and not a failure. You don't anticipate any difficulty in an environment that values teamwork, rewards initiative, provides an appropriate opportunity for advancement, achieves its goals and is a congenial place to work.

What are three things you are afraid to find in this job?

Reply: Your only concern is that you have the opportunity to excel and that research has revealed this is the place to achieve it.

How do you motivate people?

Reply: 'The best motivator is the one that comes from within. Threats are perverted and misunderstood. Fear works sometimes but not in every situation. Peer pressure works best only on young people.'

Why do employers choose behavioural interviewing?

Some information about recruitment using the traditional interview process:

• 1 in 4 recruitment exercises currently end with the wrong person being recruited
• 42% of Australia's Fast 100 companies have faced unfair dismissal claims
• Nearly 50% of all employees believe they are currently in the wrong position
• The cost of a wrong hire is between .75 and 1.5 times the position's annual salary.

The cost of a misfire

You hire a store assistant who is on $25,000 pa. After eight months, this employee leaves the organisation because they are not satisfied with the work (they were not the right person for the job). How much has this bad hiring decision cost you?

Cost:

A very conservative estimate of the cost is $25,000 X .75 = **$18,750**
A more realistic cost is $25,000 X 1.5 = $37,500, and even this in many cases may be less than the real cost.

This single employee will have cost you between $18,750 - $37,500. Multiply this by every bad hiring decision, and you can see why it is necessary to improve recruitment processes, and I haven't even mentioned reduced productivity, increased staff turnover, lower morale, wasted recruitment and training costs and missed opportunities.

Tips for successful interviews

Today's highly competitive job market demands a more sophisticated approach to the interview process. The time that you spend with an interviewer may determine your career future. A successful interview is a vital step toward the fulfilment of your ambitions. This chapter will provide you with in-depth information on how to conduct yourself during an interview.

Interview preparation

Like any good business meeting, sales call or another important encounter, preparation and strategy will achieve the best interview result. Apart from basic information regarding the interviewer's name, correct pronunciation, position, company and address, as much knowledge must be gained as possible on the company's products or services, market perception, growth and culture. With this information, you will be well equipped to prepare and answer questions from a position of strength.

This information will also assist your enthusiasm for the company as a potential employer. It is also important that you prepare a list of questions to ask during the interview. Remember that the interview is a two-way street. The employer will try to determine through questioning if you have the qualifications and experience necessary for the position. You, too, must determine through questioning that the company will provide the opportunity and environment you seek. A discerning interviewer will well receive pertinent and intelligent questions.

Typical questions may include:

- Is there a detailed position description available?
- What is the reason for the vacancy?
- Is there an induction and training program in place?
- What are the key performance measures for this position?
- How and when will performance appraisals be conducted?
- What opportunities are available for the high achiever?
- What are the company's growth plans?

Preparation for the interview entails a full understanding of your strengths and weaknesses, ambitions and employment requirements. You should feel confident in discussing these areas, projecting a positive attitude and your value to an employer.

A well-prepared resume will be necessary covering personal details, education and qualifications, career history overview including employment dates, brief employer description, reporting structure, responsibilities, achievements and reason for leaving or wishing to leave.

Your image

Your image during the interview is critical. Image is very much non-verbal communication. If you do not utter a single word, the way you look will tell people a lot about you. People make many subconscious decisions based on your presentation, your economic, social and educational level and heritage, your trustworthiness, level of sophistication, success and moral character.

Add to this the fact that 90% of people will form an opinion of you within the first 10 – 40 seconds of a meeting and, in an interview, you will be virtually fully judged within the first four minutes. It has been found that the impression you create is based 55% on the way you look (dress), 38% on the way you physically present (body language) and 7% on what you say. You can see how creating a positive first impression is vital!

Your physical presence or dress should reflect the culture you are entering. Your initial company research and advice from your consultant can determine this. If in doubt, a conservative, corporate dress style such as a business suit should be adopted. Be sure all facets of your grooming and hygiene are immaculate. Posture, movements and mannerisms should be natural. Your manner of speaking should be considered so that you are clearly understood. Convey the right amount of enthusiasm, sincerity, respect and warmth. Pay attention to your listening skills and maintain good eye contact. Communicate forthrightly and credibly; organise your thoughts.

The interview

It is important to be prepared for a variety of interview styles. Not all interviewers are skilled practitioners, and you may experience considerable contrasts.

Having a basic interview strategy will allow you to adapt confidently to any style of interviewer and ensure that you can discuss your past performance, the position description, the type of person being sought, position analysis including objectives, your relevant experience, education and personal attributes.

Your strategy should include:

- Mirroring the style and pace of your interviewer
- Answering questions forthrightly and credibly without over-elaboration
- Listening carefully
- Maintaining eye contact
- Conveying enthusiasm and warmth
- Using natural gestures and avoiding nervous fidgeting
- Ensuring you speak clearly.

The interview process is two-way communication. There should be no 'hierarchal' overtone. You should feel relaxed and confident after all both you and your interviewer are meeting to find out about each other and determine whether each of you has a match.

The following list will provide you with sound interview etiquette:

- Plan to arrive on time or a few minutes early. Late arrival for an interview is inexcusable. Check with the receptionist on arrival. If presented with an application, fill it out neatly and completely
- If you have a personal resume, be sure the person to whom you release it is the one who will do the hiring
- Greet the interviewer by their surname using the correct pronunciation and salutation
- Shake hands firmly, not limply or crushingly
- Wait until you are offered a chair before sitting
- Sit upright, look alert and interested at all times
- Be a good listener as well as a good talker
- Smile alot
- Don't smoke, even if you are offered a cigarette
- Don't chew gum
- Maintain eye contact during the interview
- Follow the interviewer's leads but try to get the interviewer to describe the position and duties to you early in the interview so that you can relate your background and skills to the position
- Try not to answer questions with a simple 'yes' or 'no'. Explain whenever possible
- Tell those things about yourself that relate to the position
- Make sure that your strengths are highlighted during the interview in a factual, sincere manner. Keep in mind that you alone can sell yourself to an interviewer
- Don't ever lie. Answer questions truthfully, frankly and keep as close to the point as possible

- Don't over answer questions. If the interviewer steers the conversation into politics or economics, it is best to answer questions honestly without saying more than is necessary
- On the issue of salary and benefits, it is best not to enquire about these areas in the initial interview, but rather at the time when you are positive, the employer is interested in you. You should be well aware of your market value and be prepared to state your salary range
- Always conduct yourself in an enthusiastic, positive manner. Show interest in the position and never close the door on opportunity. It is far better to be in a position where you can choose from several positions rather than only one.

Closing the interview

If the position is of interest, let that be known to the interviewer. Ask the interviewer if what has been gleaned from the interview fits what they are looking for. This will allow you to overcome any objections they may have at this point and allow you to convince the interviewer that you are the right person for the position.

If the position is offered to you and you want it, accept on the spot. If you wish time to think it over, be courteous and tactful in asking for that time. Set a definite timeframe in which you will respond.

Don't be discouraged if no definite offer is made or specific salary discussed. The interviewer may need to communicate with others before a decision. Should you feel the interview is not going well, don't let your discouragement show. Your reactions may be being tested. Always thank the interviewer for their time and consideration. If you have provided the reasons you are interested in joining the company and given details of what you can bring to the company, then you have done the best you can. As you arrived with a smile, remember to depart with a smile!

Some typical interview questions which you may face:

- What do you know about our company?
- Why would you like to work for our company?
- Why are you looking for another position?
- What have been your major achievements?
- Describe your ideal working environment.
- What type of management style do you work best with?
- What would your current manager say about you?
- In your most recent position, what has been your most significant accomplishments?
- What motivates you in a work environment?
- What frustrates you in the work environment?
- What are your expectations of an organisation about your career objectives?
- What would you bring to this position?
- How would you describe your personality?
- What are some of your outside activities and interests?
- What are your strengths?
- What areas have you identified that you would like to improve on and what have you done about them?
- What are your career ambitions?
- What level of salary are you seeking?

Factors evaluated negatively in an interview

- Poor personal appearance
- Overbearing aggressive attitude; conceit; 'know-all' attitude
- Inability to express thoughts clearly
- Poor diction, grammar, posture
- Lack of planning for career or life – no goals or purpose
- Not showing interest or enthusiasm; passiveness and indifference
- Lack of confidence – nervousness
- Over-emphasis on money
- Evasiveness
- Lack of tactfulness, maturity, and courtesy
- Condemnation of past employer/s
- Poor eye contact with the interviewer
- Poor handshake
- Failure to ask questions about the position
- Lack of preparation for the interview.

If you have obtained the interview through an employment consultant, your feedback to the referring consultant is very important. Before talking with the client, your consultant will want to know what transpired during the interview from your perspective.

Be open about the positive and negative aspects of the interview. Advise your interest in the position and your thoughts about the client's reaction. Your consultant can greatly assist you in securing the position if well prepared before speaking with the client.

A follow-up letter to thank the interviewer for their time is an effective technique rarely used today. In a way, it reminds the interviewer who you are, and it offers an opportunity for you to restate your strengths and why you are the best person for the job.

10 Key tips for job interviews

• Establish useful contacts by using the aid of friends and acquaintances
• Do thorough homework on a company before going there
• Identify who has the power to hire you within a company and then use your contacts to set up a meeting
• Ask for a 20-minute interview when seeking an appointment with the person who has the power to hire you
• Go to your meeting with a list of questions to determine whether the job fits you
• Only talk about yourself at a meeting if it can add value to the company and its problems
• When answering a question, ensure your response is relevant and to the point. Do not talk yourself out of a job
• Present yourself as a resource person at any meeting who can produce better work than anyone before you
• Appear to be positive in life and flexible in your approach to work
Always send a thank-you note immediately after the meeting.

Advanced behavioural interview questions

Interview questions change from time to time, even though new questions are predominantly seeking similar responses or outcomes. It could be described as a 'variation on a theme' designed to ensure the recruiter maintains the 'upper hand' and element of surprise at the interview. I suppose recruiters are concerned about the same questions being utilised across many employment agencies and companies to such an extent that they become rehashed and ineffective.

To help alleviate this problem, I asked several leading recruiters in Melbourne and Sydney to provide me with their 'top questions' currently being applied today. The response was not surprising, and there was an element of consistency in the questions currently in use. The questions focused on *key competencies* or required levels of skill and proficiency expected across many companies today.

Below are the questions I collated from the responses I received from leading employment agencies. These questions *must* become second nature to you if you are to succeed at interviews.

Profitability impact
Please demonstrate a time when you have identified, developed and maximised value creation opportunities that had an impact on the profitability of the company?

Technical Skills
Please give an example of when you have used your technical skills and creativity to implement new capital works ideas to increase, improve product output and quality?

Influencing Skills
Please give an example of when you had to influence superiors, line managers or suppliers to implement a change management program. What were the main challenges you faced?

Communication
Tell me about a time when you've had to explain a technical concept to non-technical people. How did you go about it, were you successful?

Decision Making

Have you ever made a decision that you later found out was wrong? What did you do?

Why was the decision you made wrong?

Leadership

Tell me about a time when you've had to make a team decision but had difficulty due to lack of consensus. How did you deal with the situation?

What was the outcome?

Planning & Organisation

Things sometimes fall through the cracks when we get busy. Can you tell me about a time when this has happened to you, and it created a problem later?

What did you do to ensure it didn't happen again?

You will note a clear theme throughout these questions focusing on key elements of success as follows:

1. Your ability to 'add value' to the business and to demonstrate a return on investment.
2. Your ability to 'communicate effectively' with others at all levels.

Companies today are recruiting on 'attitude' as the first of their selection criteria as much as on technical experience. Employers are looking for a fit with their business values and ethics. Your ability to fit into an organisational culture is paramount, so if there is a small deficiency in technical skill, companies will close that gap with effective training and development. Recruiting on 'attitude' becomes a key factor for selection when you have two or three shortlisted candidates with the same level of technical experience.

The interviewer will probe with follow-up questions that focus on:

The situation (what specifically happened)

What was the project?

What were the circumstances?

When did it happen?

What brought this problem to your attention?

What made the situation difficult?

What you did or said

Tell me exactly what you did?

What did you do next?

What steps did you take in handling the situation?

What caused you to be so successful in this particular situation?

An example of a 'textbook' response to a behavioural interview question is as follows:

Question: 'Describe a time when you worked on a team that was having difficulties.'

Answer: 'I spent a semester working with a project team for my psychology class.'

Our assignment was...

My responsibility was...

We had difficulty because...

My reaction/thought process was...

The results were…

Assessment interview technique

I had the privilege to study an amazing and very effective recruitment technique by one of Australia's leading recruiters. This technique is used when recruiting for senior management roles, so it will not affect job seekers in positions below management level.

The interview technique is referred to as 'Assessment Interview' and is designed to determine whether a candidate is a high potential applicant for a job. It involves asking a series of well-designed questions that measure success going back to childhood. The recruiter will take almost 1.5 hours to complete this process effectively, and they will establish a set of keywords that best describe the candidate profile.

Like behavioural interviewing, the interview questions will be designed to determine your past actions or achievements and will require in-depth responses by the applicant, which requires supporting examples. The interviewer will probe the applicant deeper when necessary. The applicants are also measured against the 'critical success factors' of the business and the job specifications that are clearly defined before the interview process.

The chart below sets the quadrants in which applicants will be assessed as far as their fit. Quadrant number 3 is the 'High Potential' candidate, which represents 25% of total applicants within the profession. Quadrant number 4 is the 'Leader' candidate where your superstars belong and represent 10% of total applicants within the profession. All companies want superstars. However, they may be limited in their ability to hire them for a variety of reason which usually comes down to their capacity to pay a super salary.

High Potential Quadrant 3 25% of Candidates	Leaders of the Future Quadrant 1 10% of Candidates
No Way Quadrant 1 20% of Candidates	Easy Way Out Quadrant 2 30% of Candidates

Skills-Experience-Knowledge

Applying emotional intelligence at interviews

I recently attended a workshop in Melbourne during Human Resources Week on Emotional Intelligence (EI). What was interesting about this event, besides the topic on hand was the number of human resources professionals present. It was the most well-attended workshop throughout the whole week, and I was astonished to see the amount of interest that Emotional Intelligence conjured amongst our professionals.

Perhaps human resources practitioners can relate to this concept better than other professions due to the humanistic element that Emotional Intelligence poses as a factor of success. Another factor that is influencing human resources practitioners in taking up the concepts of Emotional Intelligence is it can be applied at the recruitment stage as a 'predictor of success' and as a measure of intelligence.

A growing body of research suggests that Emotional Intelligence is a better predictor of success than more traditional measures. It may be the single most important factor that leverages the success of people and characterises those individuals with the 'right stuff'. Research also indicates that while your IQ level contributes 20% of your success; another 36% can be attributed to your Emotional Intelligence (EI). At least 90% of the difference between outstanding and average leaders is related to Emotional Intelligence (EI) and explains why some people excel while others of the same calibre lag behind.

As a human resource professional, this breaks new ground when recruiting employees. It has been a while since any new technique or tool of such magnitude has been able to draw such interest from human resources professionals. Earlier in my book, I refer to how human resources professionals move en masse with the next craze when it comes to recruitment and selection techniques. Well, here it is, in the guise of Emotional Intelligence. Recruiters will commence changing selection criteria for vacant positions to include Emotional Intelligence (EI) competencies, and new behavioural questions will be developed to extract your level of (EI) at the interview.

Genos Pty Ltd has already developed assessments to test your level of Emotional Intelligence during the selection process.

To find out more about these testing products, go to www.genos.com.au

You may find sitting a pre-employment test to measure your Emotional intelligence amongst a suite of other tests usually conducted to measure your abilities.

What is emotional intelligence (EI)?

It is the 'street smart' or 'intuition' in you. You are reflecting your ability to deal successfully with other people, your feelings, and your everyday work and social environment.

Ever since the publication of Daniel Goleman's first book on the topic in 1995, Emotional Intelligence has become one of the most talked and written about 'influencers' of personal and business success.

Applying (EI) at interviews

When you are preparing for your interview, consider the following elements of emotional intelligence that you should demonstrate or incorporate into your answers to interview questions.

Awareness

Awareness of your own and others' emotions.

Reasoning

Understand that emotions influence learning, thinking and decision-making.

Action

Controlling strong personal emotions and reactions. Managing the emotional environment, you work in by responding to other people's emotions appropriately.

Within Australia, the most current and Australian-specific measure of workplace emotional intelligence has been developed by the Swinburne University of Technology. There are five competencies that recruiters will apply in measuring your Emotional Intelligence (EI) as follows:

Emotional recognition and expression (in oneself)

• The ability to identify one's feelings and emotional states and the ability to express those inner feelings to others
• Understanding others emotions
• The ability to identify and understand the emotions of others and how these are expressed (i.e. Students in class, at staff meetings)
• Emotions influence learning, thinking and decision-making
• The extent to which emotions and emotional knowledge are incorporated in decision-making and problem-solving
• Emotional management
• The ability to manage positive and negative emotions both within oneself and others
• Emotional self-control
• The ability to effectively control strong emotional states experienced at work such as anger, stress, anxiety and frustration.

Applying neuro-linguistic programming (NLP) at interviews

Before I attempt to explain what may appear to be a complicated area, my only purpose in raising this concept with you is to create awareness. That is an appreciation that Neuro-Linguistic Programming does have a place at job interviews and that some recruiters apply aspects of this technique in one form or another. In my experience, the recruiters most likely to utilise key aspects of NLP come from a psychology background and are naturally attracted to this technique because of its scientific approach. Other recruiters may apply aspects of it by default and without realising it because they have excellent rapport building abilities and are good at reading others (gut feel). However, they will never admit to it being NLP or any other recruitment technique for that matter.

If you want to know more about NLP, there are plenty of books on the topic. Many are complicated and seem to forget that not all people are psychologists. One book that does set it out in relatively easy-to-understand terms is by Sue Knight and is entitled *NLP at Work*. You will not find it in bookshops. However, online bookshops such as Dymocks or Amazon will carry the title.

When you are attending interviews, be aware that some recruiters may use aspects of this technique to determine your response to interview questions. Recruiters may by reading your body language, eye movements and then interpreting how this will substantiate your verbal response. I don't want to frighten anyone into thinking that a recruiter with expertise in NLP will conduct every interview they attend. Far from it, and it will be fairly infrequent overall. But like anything else in life, it doesn't hurt to know.

What is NLP?

NLP is a study of our thinking, behaviour, and language patterns so that we can build sets of strategies that work for us in making decisions, building relationships, starting up a business etc.

Neuro

By increasing our awareness of the patterns in our thinking, we can learn how these thought patterns influence the results we are getting in work and life. The key to finding personal and business success comes primarily from within ourselves and learning about how we think enables us to tap into our inner resources.

Linguistic

Our language is life. What we can say is what we can think and what we can do. Learning to master and understand the structure of our language is essential in a world where we trade increasingly through our ability to communicate. By programming, we run our lives by strategies, similar to the way that a computer uses a program to achieve a specific result. By understanding the strategies by which we run our lives, we give ourselves a choice.

Thinking patterns

If you want to get your message across at interviews, to consider the thinking patterns that you are using, keeping in mind that we are all driven by different thinking patterns. The connections you make at the interview and the way you represent them are unique to you. By understanding the way your thinking patterns influence others, you can be in greater control of the outcome of your communication and increase your effectiveness at interviews. For example, there are three main ways of thinking:

Visual

You think in pictures.

Auditory

You think it sounds.

Feelings

You represent thoughts as feelings, either internal emotions or the thought of physical touch.

You will find you have a preference for one of these ways of thinking, both in the way in which you think and communicate. At an interview, your ability to recognise your thinking patterns and maximise their effectiveness when answering interview questions can assist you considerably. Also understanding that the recruiter may also be responsive to a particular thinking pattern may help you in developing rapport and relationship.

Using your body language

Recruiters look for body language to confirm, re-affirm or to look deeper into a candidate when asking interview questions. Body language is an expression of our thinking and can tell us a lot more than you could imagine about an individual and their reaction to certain questions. A good recruiter will be good at picking up these signals and interpreting them later on. It is the ability to detect body language patterns that are unique to NLP.

Your eyes

Have you attended interviews, where the recruiter has 'fallen in love' with your eyes? Did it make you feel nervous that the recruiter continuously stared at you? Perhaps you thought they had taken a fancy to you! To make you feel more comfortable, it was probably the recruiter looking in your eyes to determine your eye movements as a response or reaction to an interview question.

Our eyes give us powerful clues to the way we are thinking. The way we use our eyes indicates the thinking that is going on. Eye movements can determine your thinking patterns, thus providing the interviewer with a greater insight into your response.

ACTIVITY FOUR

1. Practice rehearsing the behavioural questions and 20 key questions in front of the mirror
2. Repeat the same exercise, but his time record your voice while rehearsing.

Activity guide

1. Find a quiet room and sit in front of the mirror as you would at an interview
2. Look at yourself in the mirror speaking to yourself; do you see anything unusual in your expression or body language?
3. Rehearse your responses to the 20 behavioural and 20 key questions and focus on what you want to say.
4. Focus on your eye movements, body posture, seating position, head movements and other forms of expression. If you notice anything unusual in your style rectify it.
5. When replaying the recording of your rehearsal do you notice any unusual pauses or monotone voice projections? Are your responses too long, too short or incomplete?
6. Find a friend or someone close to you to provide feedback on your responses for this activity
Don't forget to smile!

ACTIVITY FIVE

Select a friend, preferably two, and arrange a rehearsal interview using the 20 behavioural questions. The interview should run between 30 minutes. Note your observations in the summary below.

Interview Summary

• Note down what you observed and what you did well at the rehearsal interview.
• Note what you observed and what you should improve.

Your Rights at an Interview

Discrimination laws apply in most western countries. In Australia, there are acts of Parliament that provide for equal opportunity and anti-discrimination laws Federally and in each State. When attending interviews, you should be aware that some questions are not permitted under equal opportunity laws. Even though most professional interviewers are aware of what not to ask candidates at interviews, you may encounter the odd inexperienced interviewer who does ask these inappropriate questions.

Discrimination

Discrimination during the interview process may occur if questions that make specific reference to the following areas are used:

- Age
- Disability or Impairment
- Industrial activity
- Marital status
- Physical features
- Political belief or activity
- Pregnancy
- Race
- Religious beliefs or activities
- Sex
- Sexual preference
- Family responsibilities
- Breastfeeding
- Criminal record
- Status as a parent or carer

• Personal association with a person identified with the above attributes.

In Australia, an employer must not discriminate against any person as follows:

• In determining who should be offered employment
• In the terms on which employment is offered to the person
• By refusing or deliberately omitting to offer employment to the person
• By denying the person access to a guidance program, apprenticeship training program or another occupational training program.

Discriminatory questions

A good test to apply during the interview process is;
Does this question have to do with my ability to do the job?'

Remember that employers must hire on merit. Below are some possible discriminatory questions you may face during the interview process.

• Is that an Irish (whatever nationality) name?
• What does your partner do for a living?
• When is your birthday?
• Do you have any physical disabilities?
• What is your economic status?
• Do you have Aids?
• Have you ever applied for or received workers compensation?

- Do you have a police record?
- Do you belong to any political organisation?

When you are asked any of the above questions at an interview, you have three main choices for responding:

- You can refuse to answer the question based on law within your country or state
- You can be pragmatic and provide answers you feel would not hurt your chances at the interview while tactfully side-stepping questions you think may diminish your chances
- You can adopt a little of 1 and 2.

If you are offended deeply by the discriminatory questions, you may report the activity to the Equal Opportunity Commission as a complaint; however, your ability to succeed in the position you have been interviewed for is probably unlikely and untenable due to the situation. This is always going to be a question of personal choice in terms of how you wish to deal with the situation.

My attitude is that if a company representative has asked you discriminatory type questions at an interview, the company is probably not worth working for. You should use this information usefully and move on to the next company. There are plenty of companies out there that are prepared to run a proper recruitment and selection process. The key goal here is to get a job and improve your job search skills. If you wish to pursue this type of distraction and you are deeply offended by the interviewer, then it is your personal choice whether to take action.

For further advice on such matters go to;

www.humanrightscommission.vic.gov.au/

humanrights.gov.au/

Age discrimination

The government extended anti-discrimination legislation to incorporate age. Age discrimination laws are designed to protect both older and younger people from discrimination in many areas including recruitment, training, promotion and redundancy or retirement.

The legislation outlaws both *direct* and *indirect* discrimination.

When someone is treated less favourably because of his or her age, *direct* discrimination has occurred.

Indirect discrimination occurs when unnecessary conditions are set, such as requiring a high level of fitness when the job does not require it, therefore disadvantaging certain people.

It is, however, possible to discriminate on the age when the inherent requirements of the job are the basis for discrimination. For example, it would be acceptable to require applicants for a gym instructor to undertake rigorous fitness testing because the job requires a high level of fitness.

Another example is an organisation with a commitment to hiring the best person for the job. As such, they will not be employing a workforce of fifteen-year-olds because they are cheaper. Instead, they will be employing the person who is most suited to the position: whether they be fifteen or fifty does not apply.

Exceptions for employment

• There are some exceptions in the legislation that relates to employment.
• It will still be legal to discriminate based on age where the inherent requirements of the job require so:
• Discrimination is still allowed to comply with industrial awards or workplace agreements
• Youth wages will still be permitted to allow young people to retain a competitive position in the labour market.

Positive discrimination

Positive discrimination is still allowed in Australian law. Positive discrimination refers to the favourable treatment of a particular age group, to meet a particular need for people of that age group to rectify disadvantage suffered by that age group, or to provide fair and legitimate benefits to people of that age group.

An example of positive discrimination is the work for the dole scheme, which focuses primarily on increasing the job prospects of younger people.

Privacy Laws and their effect on recruitment

Companies must now comply with the Privacy Amendment Act legislation, which is designed to protect the personal information of individuals. This has an impact on how companies process your personal information during the recruitment process.

Privacy legislation will affect how companies:

- Collect personal and sensitive information
- How that information is used
- How it is disclosed
- How it is stored and when it is destroyed
- How candidates access it.

Personal information can be defined as information or an opinion, recorded in any form, whether true or not, about an individual whose identity is apparent or can reasonably be ascertained.

Sensitive information can be defined as information about an individual's racial or ethnic origin, political opinions, membership of political associations, religious beliefs or affiliations, philosophical beliefs, membership of a profession, trade or trade union, sexual preferences or practices, criminal records and health information.

What if you left a job in difficult circumstances?

This area is one of the most difficult aspects of job search advice. This is because most job search literature does not make any real attempt to cover the topic in any detail. I am certain this is due to the lack of experience of authors and so-called experts in the career development profession. It is one of those topics that unless you have been through it yourself or have seen the unfortunate consequences of it, it is unlikely you are in a position to provide any proper advice.

I want to spend some time on this topic because I feel it is where I can provide the greatest assistance. I also know that people who have left their jobs in difficult circumstances are in a vulnerable position as far as their job search is concerned. This is because employers secretly do not like candidates who are unemployed unless there is a really good reason for it. This adds a lot of pressure to unemployed candidates because not only do they need to win that job and compete with others who are employed, but they also need to justify their current state of unemployment carefully.

If there is any solid advice, I can give you, it is to look for a job while you are still employed. The contradiction here is that people do lose their jobs for many reasons. In this section, I will assist you on this basis and provide you with advice to get through this difficult period in your life. There are many reasons why people leave their jobs. In some cases, it may be in difficult circumstances such as:

- Redundancy or retrenchment
- A fall-out with your boss
- Restructuring of duties
- Serious misconduct
- Poor performance
- Taking a break (sabbatical)
- Personal issues
- Health
- Not an organisational fit.

Whatever the circumstances are, you must not lose faith in your abilities or lose self-confidence. This is easy to do when you leave a job in difficult circumstances because we can be very hard on ourselves. You will go through a process of self-doubt and rejection – constantly questioning your role in having lost your job and what you could have done to redeem the situation or prevent it from happening. Just remember this, once you leave an organisation in difficult circumstances it is over!

No matter what you do now, you cannot change what has happened rightly or wrongly. You must leave it be and move on.

The best you can do is learn from your experience. If you have been made redundant, for example, then the decision was out of your control, and there was probably nothing you could do about it. Don't blame yourself for decisions you did not influence. Companies are restructuring all the time today, and it is a normal part of the business. You will have to come to terms with this and accept it as a part of the working landscape. If your boss has told you that things are not working out because you are not a fit, then don't take it personally.

You may have been good at what you do; however, organisational cultures can be complex and sometimes we can be different for a variety of good reasons.

My friend Daniel was unhappy in his job and decided to make a brave decision and leave his position to look for something else. He resigned his job with nothing to go to. People thought he was mad for doing this, but I advised him he was brave for leaving a situation that was not working for him. Daniel had confidence in himself and his abilities, and he never gave up on his desire to get another job. With some job search advice and fine-tuning of his resume, I was able to assist him in getting another job and guess what? It was a better-paid job in a larger organisation.

His move had paid off for him. I acknowledge his success to be based on self-confidence and letting go of the past. Daniel had also accepted the reality of his current situation and was able to develop a script for interviews that ensured he was able to sell his reasons for leaving to potential employers and employment consultants. Daniel had left in difficult circumstances. However, he was able to make it work with a proper job search strategy.

Have you been fired for serious misconduct?
This will be a very difficult situation for you if you have been dismissed for the following:

- Fraud
- Theft
- Physical abuse
- Intoxication
- Neglect for health and safety
- Sexual harassment
- A serious breach of company policy and procedure.

I can assure you that once you have committed serious misconduct in any organisation and been found guilty after an intense internal investigation, your career as you know it is over! The word will get around amongst fellow professionals, and you will be branded. This, of course, will never be acknowledged by others or companies alike. The shroud of secrecy will remain because companies do not want litigation for defaming someone in public.

So, it all happens behind the scenes and in a veil of secrecy. How do I know all of this?

This is where my human resources experience comes into it; I have seen it happen many times. There is no such thing as total confidentiality when more than one person is involved. I have always held a rule of thumb that if the information about your dismissal is available to more than one person, then it will get out. Despite what others say to you, there is no such thing as total confidentiality.

I remember receiving a phone call from an employment agency advising me of a person working in the finance department who was being investigated by the police for fraud. This employee was hired on contract for six months only.

There was no conviction at this stage, and the police would not provide any detailed information because they were not sure whether the matter would be taken further. What do you think the company did when they found out? You guessed it; they terminated the contract of employment and paid the contract out.

The company thought of some downsizing excuse when it was explained to the employee. There you have it, a real example of a company not taking any risks with a person with a suspected tainted past.

Your best option here is to take on a new career path quickly as far away as possible from any connection to your previous profession. You may have a hobby that you are good at and can develop further or perhaps you want to start your own business or franchise in a separate industry. If you can afford it, going back to school to study something different altogether may launch a new career.

The worst-case scenario is that you have a very close friend or relative who can assist you with a job and give you another chance in life. Whatever you decide, you must leave your old profession and start again because the stigma of what you have done will remain for a long time.

This is the cruel reality of life, and I say this to you because I have experienced this situation as a human resource professional in many large companies on countless numbers of occasions. The bottom line is that no matter how good you are if your integrity has been severely damaged, then you will be deemed a risk to the business and employers will not hire you.

Are you currently employed with the most current company listed on your resume?

If your answer to this question is no and you were fired –

Reply: *'My boss and I didn't get along, and I have to admit I didn't handle the situation very well. We had vast differences in style and opinion. I'm someone with a lot of initiative who likes to be trusted to do a good job. My boss was highly structured and autocratic and maintained a high level of control. He did not like to delegate. However, I have learned my lesson, and I should not have spoken to him as I did'.*

Why are you thinking about leaving your job?

If you are unhappy in your current job, never speak badly about your current or past employers. Be positive and make it clear that you are seeking more responsibility, a bigger challenge and greater opportunities for growth.

Reply: *'There is a great deal I enjoy about my current job. But my potential for growth in this area is limited because of the size of the company and the fact that expansion is not part of its current strategic plan.'*

Looking back on your experiences do you think there was anything you could have done to improve your relationship with your previous boss?

Use this question to demonstrate your maturity in terms of experience and dealing better with difficult people.

Reply: *'Of course, I do. The work experience I have had since has shown me how to accept criticism better. Now I understand the pressures my supervisors are under, and I can anticipate their needs.'*

Why were you dismissed?

Whatever you say, don't advertise that you were dismissed: If you are asked, be honest and answer in a way that you can turn a negative into a positive response.

Reply: *'I'm sorry to say, but I deserved it. I was having some personal problems at the time, and I let them affect my work. I was getting to work late, and I had lost all motivation.'*

Tips on answering difficult questions

- Be positive about leaving your job
- If you were fired, stress what you have learned from the experience
- Never speak badly of past employers or bosses
- Provide examples of confidence that other employers have placed in you
- Be honest, play up your strengths and don't provide negative information voluntarily
- Keep your answers brief and answer questions directly
- Believe in yourself and stand by your decisions for leaving or wanting to leave your job

- Don't advertise your difficult situations upfront; wait until you are asked the question.

Your Projection and profile

In my introduction to this book, I indicated how critical it is today for employers to ensure they can achieve a quality match during the recruitment process when screening possible candidates. Your projection and profile may be the only thing left standing when applicants of equal ability are key contenders for a job. Your ability to align with corporate values and mission statements is essential. Companies will want you to be an extension of their corporate profile, and you will be measured on your ability to fit that mould.

If you can obtain information on the corporate values of the company you are attending an interview for and can translate that into your profile, then you have a definite edge.

Research, the founder of the company and what type of person they are. See if you can obtain articles on the company and write-ups on the CEO. Is the company older, traditional and more conservative, or is it a new, vibrant and entrepreneurial business? Do your homework and get that edge on other candidates.

You will be asked questions at interviews that seek to project your personal, business and professional profiles. Employers are always interested in your profiles as part of trying to establish a key match. For example, does your professional profile match the organisational profile and corporate culture? Here are questions you may encounter that focus on your profiles:

- How would you describe yourself?
- How would people you work with describe you?

- How would your superiors describe you?

During the interview process, try wherever practicable to reflect on your personal and professional profiles in your responses to interview questions.

Personal Profile	Professional Profile
Reliability	Drive
Honesty	Motivation
Pride	Communication skills
Dedication	Team-player
Analytical skills	Energy
Listening	Confidence
Integrity	Determination

During the interview, it is good practice to add to your personal and professional profile by reflecting on your business profile. Your business profile is an indication of your work ethics. Companies are always interested in the prospective candidate's work ethics and will consider various behaviours, such as getting to work on time and working late if required.

Interviewers will test your ability to get tasks done more efficiently and economically by thinking of improved ways of doing things. Companies also have rules and standards called procedures, and they expect employees to follow these rules all the time while performing their daily activities. The bottom line is about money and companies are profit-making organisations, so your ability to contribute to business profit maximisation will be considered positively by employers.

Build your business profile into your answer to interview questions wherever possible. The following is a list of the key business profiles you should consider:

Efficiency

Organisations are interested in return on investment today. In most cases, employees are doing the work that traditionally 1.5 or 2 people performed. With the advancement in technology and rationalisation of business processes, this has meant an expectation for greater efficiency in the workplace.

When responding to interview questions about your skills and achievements, reflect how you have made a process or task cost-effective by being more efficient. This could mean reviewing the current process and finding new advancements in how to perform a task with fewer resources, time and effort. Use specific examples of when you sought greater efficiencies and the part you played in achieving your goal.

Also, don't be shy to elaborate on the dollar costs savings or benefits to the company. Sell yourself and become better at marketing your abilities to affect the bottom line and add value to the business.

Economy

Employers like people who may hold a wider perspective on doing business and understand the broader economic realities influencing management. Understanding the economy and the influences, this has on running a business projects you as an applicant that can see things beyond your current role and the impact it may have on other positions in the company.

For example, if you are applying for a store management position, what does the demographics of your area, the importation of the generic product, legislation and current trends have on your ability to grow the business. The economy is about thinking outside the square and having a broader view beyond your current position. It's about contribution and how your knowledge can impact others and assist in growing the business.

Procedures

Companies have procedures to ensure consistency in decision-making, application and interpretation. Without procedures, there would be little security for companies to delegate and empower people to make decisions confidently. Companies like people that conform to policies and procedures and do not like employees that steer away from procedural guidelines. When answering interview questions, reflect on your application of procedures when making decisions.

A good example of this would be an employee that is going through the counselling process for poor performance. Companies do not like 'Rambo' style managers that sack their employees on the spot without going through the correct procedure. Another example would be a store manager and their authority to provide refunds to customers. Following procedures ensure companies do not end up in litigation and ensure due diligence is maintained.

Profit

This is related to our explanation on efficiency and the notion that private companies are profit maximising organisations. Companies hire employees that can contribute to the bottom line by providing a valuable service to the customer. Profit maximisation is about understanding who the customer is and your role in this process. At an interview, companies may test your contribution to the company bottom line and the impact or control you had in maintaining your budget. This is particularly important for those people employed on a commission basis or by performance. If you are not paid in this manner and earn a wage or salary, demonstrate your effect on the bottom line by ensuring customers are satisfied or where you have delivered excellent service in current or past positions. Showing an understanding that private companies need to make profits, and your role in achieving this aim is important when answering interview questions.

Wrapping-up the interview

The interview has gone well, and you are getting signals from the interviewer to wrap it up. A word of caution, you are not in the clear yet. The interview is not over until you have departed from the premises. As strange as this may seem to you, an experienced interviewer will continue to assess and measure you as a suitable candidate even after the formal interview is over. This technique is very subtle, and you may not notice it.

Signals for wrapping-up

The interviewer will generally signal the conclusion of the interview with a series of wrapping up questions as follows:

Do you have any questions you wish to ask about the job?

If your answer is no, then pack your bags and go home. Getting this job may be one of the greatest opportunities you have been looking for. If you have no questions, then you have substantially reduced any opportunity of getting the job.

Asking questions

There are many questions you can ask an interviewer during the formal interview. The benefits are that it increases dialogue and assists in marketing yourself more actively. You are demonstrating you have researched the business and you are assessing whether the company is the right one for you.

All interviews are a process of two-way communication where both parties are actively selling each other. You should engage in this process actively. Here are examples of questions and techniques you can use:

• Study the company balance sheet to determine profitability. If there are abnormal losses, raise them at the interview by seeking clarification
• Seek information on career planning. Are there opportunities to diversify your skills into other areas? Find out what are the traditional paths for promotion
• Clarify the company mission and its short to long-term objectives Ask why and how the position became vacant.

More demanding questions to ask

The following questions are more probing and therefore demanding for you to ask. It is recommended you measure the relationship you have established with the interviewer before you ask these questions.

- Every company has its strengths and weaknesses, what are they for your company?
- What is the most common reason for people leaving this company?
- Give me an idea of what my potential boss is like?
- What goes into making people successful in this company?
- How has this vacancy come about?
- Is travel involved? If so, how frequent is it?
- Will relocation be necessary for the future?
- Is there a need for further education in future? If so, will the company sponsor it?

Exit gracefully

Remember that the interview is not over until you have departed from the premises. Pay attention to your manner when you wrap-up the interview.

- Shake hands firmly with the interviewer and others present on the interview panel
- Always thank them for the opportunity of being interviewed and their time
- Remember the first name of the interviewer and don't be shy to use it during the interview
- Always attempt to make eye contact
Smile as much as possible.

Tips on questions not to ask

• Don't ask about salary or benefits until you are offered the job or it is raised at the interview

• Don't ask about time off until you are offered the job

• Don't seek an early decision from the interviewer

• Don't show discouragement if the interviewer is showing no signals of whether or not they are pleased with your responses.

ACTIVITY SIX

The pressure interview

This is the ultimate of all interview practice sessions. If you can complete this activity, then no one can stop you from achieving interview success! Here are your guidelines:

- Find three friends or relatives to help you
- Find a quiet place with a table big enough to seat four people
- The aim is for your friends to bombard you with questions, one after the other, from questions contained in this book
- The entire interview should take no longer than thirty minutes
- Your friends must be assertive and apply pressure on you
- ..There must be a debriefing session afterwards to discuss your responses and your general performance

Try the pressure interview sessions more than once to improve your skill.

Write your debriefing notes on the interview outcome.

A Job Monitor Record

Application #1	Actions	Outcomes
Accounts Clerk	Company XYZ	Package: $50,000
	Sent:	12/12/2018
	Received	18/01/2019 reject
	1st Interview meeting	
	Outcome	
	Sent follow-up letter	
	2nd Interview meeting	
	Sent 2nd follow-up letter	
	Outcome	
	Interviewer Name/s	
	Interview Comments	

4 HOW TO INCREASE YOUR SALARY PACKAGE

This chapter will always come back to a fundamental point, and that is why are you leaving your job? If you are leaving because you feel ready to move up the next step and achieve greater things, then this chapter will be most appropriate to you.

You may feel as though you are starting to stagnate and that you have achieved all you can in your current role; there is no opportunity for advancement and that the only way up is to leave. You have performed well and done a good job to date and have developed some excellent skills in the market place.

You may have heard of others performing similar roles, getting paid more than you and you have established that the market rate is higher than your current rate. You feel perhaps undervalued and want more.

These are perfectly good reasons to leave a company and try somewhere else. My attitude has always been that if it becomes apparent that what you want is not available in your current organisation within a reasonable time frame, then there is nothing wrong with packing your bags and leaving. I would describe a reasonable time frame in a company as 2–5 years depending on the industry.

The art is really in being able to find something better before you leave your current role. Employers hold greater value when you are looking for work if you are currently employed. It's psychological, that is, it is perceived that you are of value to another organisation so you must be employable.

I believe that it has to do with someone already wanting you, so it is all right for another company to want you more. It also puts you in a better bargaining position for salary negotiations later on. If you are in this bracket, then you are a contender for a higher salary package within six weeks of at least 10%.

Only in exceptional circumstances have I seen employees increase their package under the following circumstances:

- The economy is moving into or is already in a recession
- The unemployment rate is rising steadily
- You have left your job unexpectedly
- You have been sacked
- You are in career transition mode
- The industry you specialise in is not performing compared to the rest of the market
- Your profession is suffering from an oversupply of candidates
- You are a new entrant into the job market and do not have at least 2 – 3 years of work experience.

Negotiating your salary

If you are on the verge of securing another position in a different organisation, then you are probably in a position to negotiate your package up by at least 10%. This is on the basis that your new role is on a comparable basis or perhaps senior to the one you perform now. I say this because you must take advantage of two things:

1. Market value for your profession
2. The initial type of interest in you.

One key point to remember is that once you accept a new role and enter an organisation, your ability to secure higher wages is diminished. You will fall back on the organisation's performance appraisal and salary review process. My advice is that the best time to secure a more substantial increase is at the negotiating table before you accept a new job. You are in the best negotiating position at this time, and it is unlikely a similar negotiating position will arise once you are employed.

Let's look at the market value initially. Every job has a band in terms of market-rate, and you could cut that band into four parts. Your knowledge, experience, industry, location and market labour economics. That is, supply and demand will determine your positioning on the higher and lower end of the band.

This is a bit of a handful, but you should be aware that jobs in the city would pay better than country regional positions for similar jobs. Also, that your position on the band may vary between industries as some industries pay better than others because of the market segment they are in an. So there are many factors you must weigh up to determine your position on the band.

A quick and easy way to determine your market value is to get a hold of expensive salary surveys and reports. Employer associations, larger employment agencies and private organisations such as the Hay Group prepare such salary surveys. The problem with this is that the majority of this information is not free, particularly if you want it to be up-to-date and specific to your position.

These reports are updated regularly and show movements in

market rates by classification based on several factors. This is the information the professionals have when determining your rate during the interview process. Another cheaper way for you to determine market rates is to look for job advertisements in your profession and establish your market salary band. I find that sometimes this is even more accurate than the salary surveys and a truer reflection of the market place. When investigating your market rate, talk to employment consultants who are privy to this information.

Develop an information base dependent upon location, experience, industry, benefits and salary to form your market rate. In other words, educate yourself as you would when buying a car or a home to establish market rates. This is important when negotiating salaries because you do not want to sell yourself short.

A good resource to get up-to-date salary survey information is contained at the Hays Consulting Web Site.

http://www.hays.com.au/salary/index.asp

Here you can search for industry average salary information for your profession. The service is called Salary Check, and it contains a Salary and Recruitment Survey.

Another excellent web site with Australian wages and salary information worth visiting:

http://www.wages.com.au/

The following table is a good example of a salary band for an accounts payable clerk. Notice the band split into four quartiles with accompanying rates of pay for those quartiles. Try to establish which quartile you are located in and then try to move to the next quartile during salary negotiations. It is not unusual for a successful candidate to move up two quartiles dependent on industry and other factors.

Your ultimate goal is to reach quartile 4 and then look at promotion to a more senior position such as accounts payable manager.

Salary band

Quartile 1	Quartile 2	Quartile 3	Quartile 4
On Commencement (1month-12months)	Some experience (1-3 years)	Experienced (3-5 Years)	Achievable Salary Target (5 years+)
$22,000-$24,000	$24,000-$25,500	$25,500-$27,000	$27,000-$29,000

Salary packaging

Many people enter salary negotiations without an appreciation of salary packaging. Salary packaging can be defined as a system for payment that is built on several reward type components.

For example, if you are on a base salary of $60k per annum, you may receive $40k in cash, $15k in the form of a lease vehicle and the remaining $5,000 split into a leased computer or medical benefits insurance. There may be some benefits associated with working in a particular company that is on top of your salary packages such as staff discounts, product rations and in-house facilities such as a gymnasium.

When negotiating your package, take all these components into account. The reason I suggest you do so is that you may receive an offer for the same base monetary amount; however, you may receive other benefits that will increase the value of your total salary package. The general term used for receiving other rewards instead of a salary amount is salary sacrifice. When you are salary sacrificing, the company provides you with an option to receive your rewards or payments in other ways besides just cash.

Here are some examples of items that can be salary sacrificed:

- Lease vehicle
- Lease computer
- Superannuation top-up
- Mobile phone
- Education expenses
- Shares or options.

Here are examples of benefits that are on top of salary packaging

- Company product rations
- Staff discount card
- Gymnasium
- Education and training sponsorship

• Options to purchase shares.

The benefit of salary sacrificing is related to payment of tax in Australia. When you are salary sacrificing you will incur Fringe benefits Tax, which is less than PAYE Tax. This is particularly useful to those in the higher income tax bracket who will end up paying less tax. So, salary sacrificing has some tax benefits for the individuals on higher salary levels; however, the limited advantage to those on less than $50k per annum as a guide. However, it is always best to check with an accountant if you are unsure of the effect this arrangement will have on your income levels or finances.

After the interview

The employer is showing signals that they may be interested in you as a credible applicant. One way to recognise this is an early indication of salary expectation.

The employer may ask you '*What is your salary expectation for this position?*'

The key point here is never to disclose your current package. Now, I am not asking you to be dishonest but to recognise that your current rate may be less than the market average. Your position or perhaps the industry you work in is not at the top end of payers for your classification. Here is an opportunity for you to provide the interviewer with your expectation of salary. Remember that we are talking about your expectations and not what you currently earn.

Increase your current rate by 10% and inform the interviewer of your new rate. Ensure that your expected salary rate does not exceed the top quartile of the market rate. So whatever you do, don't price yourself out of the market and get too greedy. Employers are aware of market rates, and if you are above the top quartile, then it is unlikely they will negotiate with you except in rare circumstances. This usually occurs when there is an undersupply in the market place, and you are a critical resource to the business. A word of caution—remember what I said in my introductory paragraph about situations in which you may not be able to achieve this at all depending on a variety of circumstances.

Increasing your salary package on the following basis may prove difficult, and you should consider seriously whether this chapter might be of assistance. Only in exceptional circumstances have I seen employees increase their package under the following circumstances:

- The economy is moving into or is in a recession
- The unemployment rate is rising steadily
- You have left your job unexpectedly
- You have been sacked or fired
- You are in career transition mode
- The industry you specialise in is not performing compared to the rest of the market
- Your profession is suffering from an oversupply of candidates
- You are a new entrant into the job market and do not have at least 2 – 3 years of work experience.

There is always an element of hype when employers have made a decision that you are the right candidate. They have purchased a new commodity of the labour market shelf, and they are pleased to have secured your employment. They are excited about you and want to sell you to the business as soon as they can as a good catch.

This initial stage of excitement is the best time to negotiate because they want you and they don't want to go through the process again. Be careful not to negotiate though over, because if you are dealing with a real pro in the recruitment business, they will have a second candidate as a backup. The back-up candidate has not been advised that they have been unsuccessful at this stage. So, don't get too greedy during this stage, look for a band of between 5 – 10% increase in your previous package. On a $50k job that is a $2,500 – $5k increase. So, use this initial hype to your advantage to secure a better deal.

The job offer

You have been successful, and you are pleased with your job offer or package. You will now receive your letter of offer or contract of employment from the employer.

Never resign from your current position until you have this offer in writing. The letter of offer is your legal contract of employment. You have worked hard at negotiating your terms and conditions of employment, and you should not give anything away now.

Check that everything you have negotiated is in the letter of offer, e.g. rates of pay and any other negotiated benefits. A key clause in the contract that you should be aware of outlines your salary and any other monetary benefits. If this clause is absent or vague, then you have a big issue with the content of the Contract of Employment.

At common law, once your terms and conditions are noted on the contract and signed by both parties, then it is set in stone. Should the employer not deliver those terms on commencement, you can take legal action at common law for breach of contract.

The contract will be binding verbally in the initial stages; however,

I still recommend that you get your letter of offer before resigning from your current employment. Even though this is rare and most employers will not do this, I have seen smaller and more unscrupulous employers change conditions upon commencement of employment. Make sure you have a valid Contract of Employment before fully accepting any job offer or resigning from your position. If you do not understand the terms of your contract of employment, get someone to help you and immediately seek clarification from the company that has made the offer.

5 YOUR CAREER OPTIONS

Keeping Your Existing Job

I felt it important to introduce this topic because performance at work can be responsible for many people suddenly deciding to switch careers, leave their place of employment and engage in a job search. Many career counsellors will not mention anything on this topic because they lack the knowledge and expertise to discuss it with confidence.

This area is difficult and requires on the job experience and knowledge in employee relations to provide proper advice. It is also a failure of many career authors to comment on job search knowledge without looking at the circumstances in which job search became an issue in the first place. With the constant pressure on companies to perform at a higher level each year and the expectations this places on employees, this means the stakes are much higher today than 20 years ago.

Employers' expectations of performance can be very sophisticated and aggressive. Employers can approach performance in this way because there is a diminishing supply of good jobs and an oversupply of good candidates. Employers are in the box seat, and if you are not performing to expectations within a reasonable time frame, then the poor performance management process will be initiated without fail.

The bottom-line today is you either perform your job well, or you are out!

If you are currently in the early stages of this process, then you need to take some action. The following points outline your options during the initiation of the poor performance process:

• Deciding if and when to commence your job search strategy
• How to ensure the poor performance process is above board and valid
• How to recognise and delay the process so that you can bite for time and get another job before it becomes too late
• Recognising that you do have performance issues and that you need to improve yourself
• Acknowledging that you are in the wrong career and workplace environment.

My experience in dealing with poor performance issues at work is that they are not always negative. Sometimes employers can be right, and through well-designed performance measurement tools have detected some issues with your performance. These performance measures are related to acceptable levels of behaviour and performance usually documented in a variety of objectives and measures, position description, performance appraisals, core values and company standards and procedures.

Most companies are well aware of the risk of litigation through unfair dismissal applications by disgruntled employees and will approach poor performance management in a very detailed and decisive way. They hire people like me to deal with difficult performance matters and to coordinate any contingencies for protecting the company. So you are getting it from the source, and I am sharing all my knowledge with you to assist in better managing your performance at work.

I have provided you with some possible scenarios or options above. How you determine which course of action to take will depend on your knowledge of the poor performance process, your circumstances and your rights and obligations at law. Hopefully, after this chapter, you will be in a better position to decide which path to take. Either way, a greater understanding in this area will assist you better manage your job search strategy and career options.

Improving your performance at work

I want to define poor performance management in the following way:

Performance management is nothing other than an approach to managing people and their potential to contribute to the business objective.'

This signifies a positive view usually adopted by most companies that poor performance management is really about rectifying poor performance and driving the correct behaviours through the company. Current methods in dealing with performance issues are to coach and mentor an employee to overcome their shortcomings and improve their performance through corrective action. This can be done in a variety of ways as follows:

Enhanced level of training in particular areas of knowledge and experience

• More regular contact and discussion on progress

- Closer monitoring through enhanced coaching by an experienced person
- Employee assistance counselling if the problem originates from issues outside the workplace
- Determining if other career options are better suited to the individual.

Most respectable and larger organisations have the expertise to manage poor performance management in the house in this manner. An important point to note is that an employer is very reliant on you to acknowledge your areas requiring improvement and to develop a partnership in formulating a plan to overcome any performance issues.

So, there is a sense of responsibility and onus on you to take control and acceptance of what is happening around you. This is why in the previous page, I prompted you to consider some possible scenarios of which one of them involves exercising your job search option.

If you are not happy in your current position and feel that the environment or culture of the company you work with is not for you, then you need to make a decision soon and deal with the issue. This is why your performance at work can have a strong bearing in terms of whether you decide to enter the job market.

Performance at work carries with it some obligations for both you and your employer. Your obligations can be summarised as:

- Your fidelity and confidentiality
- Your obedience and co-operation
- Your care and skill.

Your fidelity and confidentiality can be governed by confidentiality agreements and policies that preside over your business conduct while your obedience and co-operation are bound by your duty statement or position description and company policies and procedures.

Care and skill are required in not engaging in reckless behaviour that can be of danger to you, co-workers and the public. When you do not uphold these obligations, it may lead to poor performance management and misconduct. So poor performance can be better defined as follows: Breach of employment obligation that fails to meet the requirements of the position.

What employers need to consider when identifying poor performance
Employers are very much aware that a poor performance process not conducted fairly and reasonably may lead to the employee challenging it through litigation. Particularly if the poor performance process, unfortunately, ends in the termination of employment for the employee. Employers are also aware that during litigation, the applicant's legal representative will test the poor performance process for errors in procedure and inconsistency in the application. An employee that is going through the poor performance counselling process must ensure that the employer has acted in the following manner:

- Been consistent
- Being reasonable
- Has collated evidence
- Considered noise factors.
  Employers must be consistent in their application when

considering or identifying poor performance issues. It is an application of a key Australian principal of behaviour when it comes to 'a fair go all-round'. That is, everyone must be treated in the same manner and have the same opportunity to defend their actions when being assessed for poor performance. It is a principle that the courts of law will uphold without a doubt in this country.

Employers need to consider all actions objectively without emotion, frustration and personal biases. This form of reasonableness ensures that employers stick to the facts and substantive employee performance failings. The employer cannot be subjective or preempt any view without having seen all the facts. This also ensures that personalities are taken out of the process.

As we do not live in a perfect world, such employer standards may vary depending on the experience of the manager and the size of the organisation, particularly, as far as having specialised personnel to deal with such matters.

However, this is where you must be vigilant in ensuring that the employer has followed these basic principles. Take notes where you feel this may not have been applied accordingly and provide good examples of such. The employer must be able to demonstrate through factual evidence such as documentation and witnesses that:

- There were performance expectations
- That they were agreed or part of the role
- The employee was suitably trained
- The employee was provided with support if requested.

An employer's case in targeting an individual performance issue can be weakened considerably if they have no hard evidence of your failings. Evidence should be regularly obtained and up to date in the form of current and past performance assessments, statistical data, witness reports and other documentation.

There has to be an indication that the poor performance has been ongoing and consistently below expectations and that the employer needs to demonstrate this pattern clearly with evidence.

You can exhibit this breach in the following ways:

• Unacceptable behaviour
• Breach of company policy and procedure
• Failure to meet job requirements.

It is a requirement in some industries and industrial agreements that a union delegate or support person be present when disciplinary meetings are taking place. This representation is important for you if you need to recall certain comments and statements that were made at a later date in court. It also adds a degree of balance to the discussion, whereas employees are less likely to be aggressive or heavy-handed.

My advice to you is always to seek some form of representation, or in a worst-case scenario, at least a witness to events that can be a colleague or good friend at work. Always remember to seek clarification of the allegations and to see evidence where this is represented. After all, your job could be on the line, and you want to be clear of the issues.

Always take comprehensive notes of discussion between you and the employer representative and do not agree to be audiotaped. No law requires you to be audiotape in the workplace and employers must have your consent to do so. Sometimes employers may not provide you with your basic rights in these instances in a ploy to get as much information from you as possible. So be alert and be careful what you say during the disciplinary meeting.

The three stages of the disciplinary process

Verbal/written counselling

The verbal counselling is an informal discussion between the manager and the employee concerned. It can be written in a more formal sense and then placed into the employee file, or it can be treated like a diary or file note. Irrespective, the employer will ensure it is documented and that any important points or comments are noted for later reference. This technology forms the initial step of the disciplinary process. It is at this point where it's still possible to rectify the behaviour or poor performance as the manager and employee are not generally in conflict mode. If you are being counselled then keep a note of your meeting and what has transcribed. If your manager has made any threatening or aggressive comments to you, then make sure you have them documented. The following is a summary of the verbal counselling process:

• Used for minor poor performance
• Its aim to develop a mutual understanding of poor performance issues
• Details and data should be recorded and kept on the employee's file.

First written warning

At this point, things have started to get more serious, and the employer is formal about the process. You may note a greater degree of seriousness with a witness from management attending the meeting with you and taking comprehensive notes of answers you may provide to questions. This is to ensure that anything that is said can be backed up later on in a court of law. What you say here will also be used against you, so think before you speak.

The first written warning is for repeated poor performance and where the nature of performance is deemed to be ongoing. It's at this point that I recommend you start commencing your job search strategies and look for another job. I discuss this in more depth in the next couple of pages.

Second written warning

Two situations warrant a second and final warning:

- Repeated instances where disciplinary action has already been taken
- Instances involving serious poor performance or misconduct.

You will find the process very much the same as the first written warning.

Termination of employment

After the second written warning, companies may decide to take the process one more step further and issue a third warning or if they have a strong case, terminate the employee's employment. Companies will weigh up the strength of their case before they terminate an employee's employment. The time frame between warnings is generally 4-6 weeks because this allows enough time for individuals to demonstrate their ability to improve.

Dismissal

The company can terminate your employment on a variety of grounds. We have already considered how it can do so under a structured disciplinary process. However, there is still the ability to dismiss your employment under certain circumstances summarily. The ability to terminate immediately without going through the disciplinary process is linked to the seriousness of the incident. The following are some examples, where depending on the severity of the incident, the company may terminate your employment for serious misconduct:

- Theft
- Drinking on the job or intoxication
- Trafficking of illegal drugs
- Industrial sabotage
- Falsifying company records
- Indecent behaviour
- Provoking or instigating a fight
- Sexual harassment
- Serious breaches of the company procedure.

The company will determine the severity of the action before summarily terminating your employment in the above circumstances. A good example of this is breaches of company policy. Let's say you breached the equal opportunity policy by downloading inappropriate material from the Internet at work of a sexual nature.

The company would be required to investigate the matter thoroughly before it decided to terminate your employment. During its investigations, it would still be required to gather hard written evidence and witness statement to determine the severity of the breach and relate it to policy and procedure. The company is also required to interview you, perhaps before and during the investigations to provide you with a right of reply and natural justice.

It is only after the company is convinced beyond doubt of the severity of the misdemeanour that it would put a recommendation for termination of employment. The company may also have an in house policy that requires you be suspended with pay and sent home while the investigation takes place.

Even if the misdemeanor is blatant and dismissible, there are still several steps in the process required before an employee can be terminated. This is based on a standard or expectation set by the Fair Work Australia and most employers know this very well. The Fair Work Act defines the circumstances in which an employee may be summarily dismissed, such as:

• Willful or deliberate behaviour by an employee that is inconsistent with the continuation of their contract of employment
• Conduct that causes imminent and serious risk to health and safety of another person, reputation, viability and profitability of an employer's business.

The Fair Work Act also provides examples in which an employee may be summarily dismissed, such as:

• Theft
• Fraud

- Assault
- Intoxication
- Not carrying out a lawful instruction.

No matter what the offence and how blatant it may be, the company still requires a valid reason for termination of employment and must apply natural justice before any termination is carried through.

There are also prohibited grounds for dismissal in Australia. The Fair Work Act defines when it is illegal to terminate an employee's employment. The following circumstances are not valid reasons to terminate employment:

- Temporary absence from work due to illness and injury (you must have medical evidence)
- Discrimination grounds
- No valid reason.

My advice to you in such circumstances is to ensure you have strong representation from a union or legal representative. When you are close to being fired, you must make every attempt to defend your rights and ensure that the company has applied the correct process.

However, having worked for employers and dealt with several of these cases, there is a point when the offence is so blatant and obvious that the company goes through the motions and eventually terminates your employment for serious misconduct.

You will know yourself when this has occurred and that you are just delaying the inevitable outcome. Companies will always stand on strong ground when the offence is blatant and serious. When this occurs, your career may take a change for the worse, and it may render your unemployable in the profession or industry you worked in. I do touch on this issue in a previous chapter to assist in whichever way possible. However, your options are limited. Employers need to consider *noise factors* that may be affecting your performance. These are outside influences such as family issues, language difficulties, illness and injury, drugs and alcohol abuse, financial difficulties and gambling.

An employer should be somewhat sympathetic here and try to assist you through this tough period with an employee assistance program; however, be aware that this assistance is not compulsory and will not last forever. So, at some point, the company is going to expect a return to normal levels of performance.

Understanding the three stages disciplinary process

If you are performance counselled at work, then it is most likely the company is applying the three stages disciplinary process to your counselling. There is no law on disciplinary processes in Australia, so what companies follow in practice is either agreed to with unions or accepted as a standard practice.

They know perfectly well that if the disciplinary process does not demonstrate, a fair goes all round and apply natural justice, then they are doomed later in court. Some of the remedies that may be handed down by Fair Work Australia are either reinstatement, compensation in the form of a payout or both.

Companies do not generally like litigation because it is a costly process and that it can grab media attention if the case is compelling enough to make good news.

Understanding the process

There is a process that most companies will follow when going through the disciplinary procedure. You should be familiar with this process because it will help you determine whether you have been given a fair go all round. The process can be defined in 6 steps as follows:

• Investigate the poor performance or specific incidence, and look for evidence to substantiate the claim
• If the evidence is appropriate and can stand in a court of law, then draft the terms of the warning letter
• Discuss the poor performance with the employee
• Consider the employee's response to the allegations and afford them the right of reply
• Consider all the circumstances
• Issue the warning letter.

Managing your career through performance management

Managing your career during the poor performance process can be very critical to your prospects. This is an area that many authors of career books do not focus on at all. There is no question that this area of employee relations can be difficult to provide advice unless exposed to it. I have been fortunate enough to work in this area for some time and have learned how employers generally behave when coping with such difficult employee matters. Despite what the literature says on performance management, employees that are being counselled for poor performance, irrespective how minor the situation, will not progress to senior levels of management.

Employers will be comfortable in just providing you with that special task or duties; however, behind the closed-door discussions, your future viability has already been determined. Once you develop any reputation for wrongdoing or performing at an inferior level, it will stick like mud. This is a reality of life in business whether you like it or not or think it unfair. What employers project and then do are two different things.

I have never seen an employee promoted who has been managed for poor performance. I have never seen a relationship properly repaired from the damage left behind from poor performance counselling.

Most employees that decided to hack it through and remain in their positions became bitter, and some chose careers as union delegates. Many just become deadwood accepting their desperate fate in corporate life. Do you want to end up this way too?

I felt this chapter would be important to you because it does not have to be like this. You do not have to work for the same company for the rest of your life and become institutionalised by their views of you. There is also nothing wrong if there is no fit between you and the company.

I once worked as a contractor for a government utility that had a sickening culture. It was built over many years of mediocrity in management and deadwood employees keen to save and maintain their only working existence. I left after only one month, and no way was I going to work in such an organisation. I exercised my right to work in an organisation where I felt there was a pro-active and innovative culture that suited me. So, there is no shame in moving on. If you are in the early stages of poor performance counselling, then start making plans to move on to another company now and don't procrastinate.

When being performance counselled, you to have two options:

• Continue working for the same company and become branded for life
• Move on and establish a new start and a new career elsewhere.

This is not easy, and it takes guts. However, you have it within you to start again elsewhere. I have provided you with good job search skills in this book, so there is no reason why you cannot commence your job search immediately. There are other employers out there that would probably be a more appropriate fit. Your focus must change, and this means moving away from spending hours worrying about how you can overcome your poor performance counselling issues. In the majority of cases, when employers begin the poor performance counselling process, and you are at the first written warning stage, my experience tells me that at least 90% end up in a mutual or forced separation. So no matter what you do, you are just delaying an inevitable outcome.

Below is a quick strategy to get your job search started:

• Have a quick look at your career strategy and aspirations in terms of what you would like to do next
• Prepare your resume or update it to reflect your current skills and achievements to date
• Determine possible referees and establish that they are happy to act on your behalf
• Commence developing your job search skills and begin by tapping into the hidden job market

- Start attending as many interviews as possible to develop your interview style and experience
- Establish your salary expectations in the meantime.

You mustn't waste time looking for a new job when being counselled for poor performance. This is because time is not on your side. Depending on the industry you work in, the economic climate and the occupation you hold it may take anywhere from between six weeks to six months to get the right job. It is also dependent upon how much effort you put into it. I made a point very early on in this book that the best time to find work is when you are employed, not unemployed. So, use this time to your advantage and make it work for you.

Other ways of achieving self-fulfillment

We all seem to have an inherent view that our only option in life, in terms of securing income and self-fulfillment, is to find another job with another company, doing the same old thing you have become accustomed to. In many ways, it is not your fault in thinking this way. Your parents most probably taught you at a very young age about the need to have a good and secure job with a reputable company and how to maintain that secure employment for as long as possible.

It was all based around the security of income and the notion that it would provide you with the psychological comfort level needed to get through life. It was built into your value system, mapped and programmed into your subconscious without you even realising. Every once in a while, at the appropriate time, this behavioural trait will rise to the surface to control your emotions, your values and whatever direction in life you decide to take. There are other ways of achieving financial independence and self-fulfillment. It does not necessarily mean getting up at dawn and returning home at dusk each day by working for someone else.

However, I must stress that no matter what your profession in life, when you receive payment for services rendered, someone else is technically employing you. It begs the question as to what degree of autonomy or control do you have in your life in the pursuit of income and satisfaction?

Most parents never taught us about obtaining income through other means, whether it is developing your business idea, becoming a consultant, turning a hobby into a paid profession. We were never educated to think about the possibility of developing ideas as a source of secondary income or how to test these ideas before leaving our day job. We were taught to get a good job with a reliable source of income in a good company.

The purpose of this chapter is to raise your awareness of other options in life and to encourage you to explore those options. Some of these alternative options could involve some pain in the initial stage as you make the transition; however, it may pay dividends later on. So it's all about having some ideas with a medium to longer-term view. This could include mapping out your vision of where you want to be in 5 – 10 years. If you have left your job in difficult circumstances, then this chapter will be most relevant to you.

Life after redundancy

Redundancy is still one of those business activities to which our society has been unable to find alternative solutions. It is a draconian method for business downsizing and reducing costs through labour reduction.

The sad part is it always seems to happen when we least need it, during recessions or minor economic downturns. Redundancy is easy in business terms because business leaders can take action quickly by reducing heads and in the process, save their skins.

Chief Executive Officers can report back to shareholders and their board of directors that they have taken action to reduce costs by getting rid of jobs in so-called non-performing business areas.

So it is not enough that you have been whacked over the head with the news of losing your job; you now have to face a brave new world that is less inviting and most likely in an economic recession. It would be nice to pick the timing of redundancy to occur during an economic upswing, but that is only wishful thinking and will never happen.

I have always held the belief that corporations and large businesses are still not mature enough to deal with business downsizing in more creative and less harmful ways. What companies are doing better today is providing services for redundant employees such as employee assistance programs, financial advice, career transition support and better severance pay.

However, it is more likely that the possibility of media coverage and militant union intervention has more to do with company support rather than being a caring organisation. Companies today don't like negative press or to be seen as bad corporate citizens. This is probably the real driving force behind the enhanced redundancy benefits and services today.

Redundancy could be an opportunity to look at your career in a different way. Perhaps you have always needed an extra push to pursue that hobby or idea you have always thought about. You may have received a substantial payout, which may fund your idea and provide you with some financial security. Whatever the case, redundancy is not a dirty word, but rather an opportunity to extend yourself further into the next phase of your career.

Future jobs growth in the next five years

As we move into the new year, some of you are going to be reflecting on your careers. Part of the process should also be an assessment of what are the growth sectors and occupations that are going to be prominent over the next five years.

Certainly, this is also a good barometer for your current position. For example, if you are in one of the slowest growing job areas, then perhaps you should start planning your next career move now.

Phil Ruthven is a leading Australian futurist and economist. He has completed an analysis of the thirty fastest and slowest growing occupations in Australia. One key point is that they are not all technology-based. Many do not require any university education at all such as handymen, credit and loans officers and general clerks.

Ranking number one and outstripping any other growth occupation by 100 times over the past four years are office trainees followed by sales and service trainees. There are also so-called 'new age' occupations entering growth lists, including alternative health professionals such as natural therapists and massage therapists. Financial service professionals such as dealers, brokers and investment advisers are not far behind, followed by computing, property professionals and tourism jobs.

The outsourcing of jobs that people don't want to do is also a growth sector. Domestic home services such as cleaners and handymen are all in a strong growth stage. This also explains the growth in waiters, bar attendants, restaurant and catering managers. We are becoming a society that does not consider the time spent doing chores around the house to be a good use of valuable free time. Perhaps this is a sign of the times, as dual-income families strive to maintain their standard of living and busy career professionals give all to their boss in the name of success!

Ten of the thirty fastest-growing occupations during the past four years in Australia:

- Office trainees
- Sales and service representatives
- Firefighters
- Natural therapy professionals
- Podiatrist
- Aquaculture farmers
- Hospitality trainees
- Earthmoving labourers
- Other agricultural labourers
- Film, television, radio and stage directors.

The ten slowest growing occupations during the past four years in Australia:
- Court and Hansard reporters
- Footwear tradespersons
- Aboriginal health workers
- Mechanical engineering tradespersons
- Clay, stone and concrete processing machine operators
- Screen printers

- Railway labourers
- Sales demonstrators and models
- Food tradespersons
- Domestic housekeepers.

My advice is to plan your career well in advance. To consider now what you need to do to achieve a new career path or to update your skills into a growth occupation. This is because career change or updating your skills does not happen overnight and requires a good deal of hard work and consideration on your behalf. If you feel you are in a slow-growth occupation at work, look for new and other opportunities.

Sometimes the best scenario for changing careers or updating your skills can be achieved in your current workplace. Use your performance appraisal process wisely when identifying new career paths and training opportunities. Look for new career opportunities when jobs are advertised at work or consider taking on part-time studies to enhance your prospects.

The Changing Labour Market

During the last fifteen years, we have witnessed a structural change in the labour market. The traditional dynamics of the job market that we grew up with during our parents working life has all but vanished. The new labour market is different and non-traditional aspects of work structure have come to the forefront. Certainly, some of us, particularly our parents, would find this hard to comprehend. Nevertheless, it is upon us, and the better you understand it, the more successful you will be at tapping into nontraditional job markets.

Demographic shifts in the employment market

During the past fifteen years, we have seen the share of the employment market decline in the states of NSW and Victoria. The growth states are now Western Australia and Queensland, although recently Queensland has been leading this shift in demographics. This reflects the structural shift in demographics as Queensland continues to be the fastest-growing state in Australia.

High growth in part-time employment

We know that part-time employment has exploded during the past fifteen years. During this time, 55 in every 100 jobs created by economic growth has been part-time.

Part-time employment has seen an annual growth of 4.5% since 1990 and now represents 2.7 million workers or 28.5% of all jobs. It is rising almost three times faster than full-time employment. Growth industries such as retail and tourism favour part-time employment and it is more resilient to economic cycles. Fifteen per cent of total male employment is now part-time, and this is revolutionary compared to 40 years ago.

Growth in the number of self-employed persons

The event of redundancies and lack of career prospects in a more competitive job market has seen a rise in self-employed persons. Statistics show that almost 1 million Australians are categorised as self-employed, and 35% of them are skilled professionals.

Shifts in industry sectors

The fastest-growing job sectors today are retail and tourism. Retail now provides 15% of employment with tourism growing to 4.3%.

Other moderate growth industry sectors include business services, property and health. The sectors in decline are manufacturing, transport and storage, finance and insurance.

ACTIVITY SEVEN

Mapping Out Your Vision

A good technique in getting to know your career goals better is to map out your vision for the future and to extrapolate where you see yourself in 5 – 10 years from now. When we are in career transition mode, it is a good time to reflect upon what we want to achieve in life. Be open with yourself and review the sort of things that motivate you with great passion.

In just one sentence, write your vision - that is, where you would like to see yourself in 5 – 10 years from now. For example, I would like to be self-employed and running my own business successfully so that I can have more time to myself.

How will you get there?

1. Write down how you are going to achieve your vision, that is, what are your milestones going to be or what do you need to do to get there. For example, do you need more training in a particular area, equity to launch your vision, support from people close to you? Just list them below with your time frame.

2. List other interests you may have.

Make a list of all your current interests and hobbies. For example, sport, music, crafts, public speaking, politics, etc.

Going out on Your Own

If you are a professional person or qualified in a particular field, you may be in a position to start your own business or consulting practice. Much will depend upon the business you are planning to be in and the demand for such services in the wider community. I suppose the only person who understands his or her profession better than anyone else is you.

Only you can decide whether there is a market out there for you and in what capacity it exists. You must also be in a state of readiness, perhaps having reached a level of maturity and experience in your profession and having developed a network of possible future clients.

However, whatever you decide, don't go into it blindly. You must research your market sector to determine whether it is feasible. Prepare a business plan, as a tool for determining whether it is feasible for you to make this jump or transition. To be able financially to launch your business and then support yourself in the initial stages is important. Much of this will come back to your family and financial position and other support services available.

Talk to professional people such as accountants, business advisers, etc. about your idea. Whatever you do, don't just wake up one morning and decide to start your own business without having done your homework.

One way of limiting the risks of going out on your own is to test your idea first. That is, starting up slowly on the side and then testing it gradually along the way. If you are an accountant, start building up some private work on weekends, or if you are a qualified tradesperson, try picking up some work on the side and see how you go. Building up your business slowly this way will provide you with a degree of confidence, a secondary source of income and provide a vehicle for testing the feasibility of your idea before you go too deep and commit other resources.

Willem Vis, the Chairman of VIP Home Services, commenced his successful franchise business in 1972 by cutting lawns in the local area for additional income. When the amount of work became too demanding for him, he began franchising his lawn-mowing concept in 1979. It took him seven years to get to that point, and today he has a network of over 1 000 franchise businesses covering a range of domestic services. During the earlier years, Willem continued working full-time, never losing sight of his business concept. Willem experimented with the possibility of other career options in his life and was able to step outside his comfort zone.

The best time to build a business is when you are employed rather than unemployed. This is because you are not panic-stricken or in a mad rush to develop your business. Too many people jump into their own business or consulting practice after they have lost their jobs. For some, this has provided the stimulus to get out there and do what they have always wanted to do. For many others it is a rude awakening and very difficult to come to terms with. It comes back to my original thought that we are taught at a very young age to embrace security and stable employment.

Our comfort zone, when we lose our job, is shattered, and many become lost in the wilderness. Going out on your own may be okay for some when they lose their job unexpectedly; however, for others, it's very difficult unless it has been a planned event. So make this a planned career move, wherever practicable, rather than an unexpected one. Work on your career options while you are gainfully employed. Remember that you have choices.

Franchising

Franchising is an interesting concept and career alternative. It is one of the fastest-growing business sectors in Australia. It is a way for buying a proven business concept with technical and business support from the franchisor. The success rate for franchising is around 80% on average. If you have been made redundant, you may wish to invest some of your money into a proven franchise concept and start your own business. Some people even borrow a percentage of the franchise costs for tax effectiveness.

This is an option for some people that will help ease the fear of going into business on your own.
Here are some resources on franchising that may help you:

Franchising Magazine is available monthly from all newsagents
A great web site with plenty of franchise information is:

http://www.franchise.net.au

Developing your hobby

Are you good at something outside work? Perhaps you are good at making something, and many of your friends have commented at how good the product is. You may be involved in community affairs and politics and have achieved some respectability and standing within the community or association you are involved in.

You may be good at sport and have achieved some initial success at competitions, and you have plenty of potentials. Perhaps you are good at writing, painting and crafts, racing cars, share trading or playing an instrument. Whatever your hobby, they all have one thing in common, and that is you love doing it, and it is serious interest.

So, if you are going to work for income only, and find that you want to be somewhere else, perhaps your hobby can be your outlet. The benefits of developing your hobby into a fulltime profession are that you understand your hobby better than anyone else and that you have a better view as to what you are dealing with. You already know who the key players in your industry segment are, the costs involved in setting up, and probably the level of performance you require. In other words, you are already educated in your hobby and have an inside view of what may be required to succeed.

I had a neighbour who enjoyed working on cars at home. He would buy them cheap, fix them and sell them at a premium. His hobby was restoring cars with minor panel imperfections. I had a friend who was very keen on share trading and reached a level of success that enabled him to trade from home successfully.

A family friend was good at building timber pergolas and other outdoor constructions. He began building pergolas for friends and extended family to the point he had so much work that he decided to take it on full-time. My brother was interested in computer games and started a part-time small business leasing computer games to video stores. There was a market niche, and he exploited it by providing greater service to the video store owners. Today he has expanded the number of video outlets from one to five in a relatively short time.

Consider the principles as discussed earlier. That is, don't go into it blindly and do your homework first. More importantly, continue doing your hobby on the side while you are employed and see if you can establish a reasonable income flow. Always test it to the next level and see how your hobby performs. You may be pleasantly surprised by the outcome.

Developing an idea or concept

Have you got a great idea or concept and want to develop this
further? We are all good at expressing our view on how we can
improve certain aspects of our daily living but rarely act on it because
it is too hard and time-consuming. In a way, there are no perceived
immediate rewards that make it a tangible proposition.

If you have an idea or concept, why not explore its possibilities?
This does not mean having to give up your day job and spend lots of
money to develop it. You can explore the possibilities in other ways.
Try to determine in the early stages how potentially feasible your idea
is. Perhaps you can receive advice from experts in the industry and
business advisers. I call this the initial drawing and exploration stage.
This occurs before any prototype being developed.

We are conditioned from exploring new ideas and concepts
because it is a high-risk zone and not guaranteed. It reflects my
thoughts on upbringing and how we were taught to develop a secure
lifestyle before anything else. It goes against the grain for most of us
to spend lots of spare time and cash on an idea and concept that has
no guarantee of success. So we defeat ourselves before we even begin
to explore the concept. You may be sitting on the next-generation
product and have not realised. If you are successful, this idea or
concept may launch a new and exciting career for you and lead you
into another profession in life you never imagined. So try to think it
through, and give it a go. If you are not successful at the drawing
stage, then at least you have not lost your job or lots of money in the
process.

Future Jobs Growth
Technology is driving occupational change

Big-spending by households has led to jobs for the humble sales assistant growing faster than any other category, but despite this, technology is the biggest driver of change, according to new research.

Some occupations are increasingly being made redundant because of new technology, a leading demographics analyst has said, and workers should aim to 'up-skill' at least once a decade to keep their jobs.

Demographer, Bernard Salt, said his recent analysis of Australian census data revealed a significant decline in the numbers of secretarial positions in the workforce. Secretaries recorded the highest number of jobs lost in those five years.

This is not because there are fewer secretaries; it is because they are changing into new job titles such as personal assistants, executive assistants and office or administration managers. Accordingly, these occupations are among the top ten recordings, the highest growth.

The use of new technology has changed the roles of several fundamental occupations, such as secretarial positions. According to ABS census data used in the research, jobs that have been created include:

- Sales assistants for household goods, food and beverages
- Marketing managers
- Office managers
- Inquiry clerks (call centre personnel)
- General managers
- Personal assistants
- Project or program administrators.

Those occupations that have shrunk since the last census include:

- Secretaries
- Bank workers
- Commercial cleaners
- General clerks
- Electronic engineering associates
- Typists or word processor operators
- Fitters
- Stock clerks.

Salt said these results reflected the increasing mechanisation of the workplace, with digital barcoding systems replacing traditional stock clerks, ATMs and EFTPOS machines making human bank tellers unnecessary and new computer programs replacing jobs like engineering associates, general clerks and typists.

Employees in these fields need to adapt to change and move into new and expanded roles that have progressed from their current occupations. For example, Salt said it was not unusual today to find a secretarial position that also involved a worker who managed accounts, made travel arrangements, organised events, or implemented new software.

'Some jobs are being pushed forward, some are being held back while another takes over its role… and it is all technology-driven'.

'The answer is multi-skilling. And employees will have to do it at least once a decade,' he said.

IN CLOSING

Now that you have read my book, you are probably going to ask 'has the author ever found a job in six weeks?' The answer is yes, many times, but six weeks was my average – on some occasions I found a job in 4 weeks!

I was not always this good at finding work, and until I perfected my job search techniques, it took me months to secure the right job. Once I was unemployed for six months! Looking back, it was obvious that my strategies were wrong. I was making the same mistakes as everyone else. I sent in resumes by the bucket load and expected an instant phone call from prospective employers.

How could they not see my talent oozing from my resume and feel compelled to jump on the phone to arrange for an interview?

The truth was that my resume was stuck with a hundred others waiting to be fed to a hungry paper shredding machine. My interview style bordered on arrogance, I thought I was so smart that only other people needed job interview help. Things changed when I decided to leave my job many years ago for a sabbatical to rediscover myself and to re-establish my career.

I knew then that prospective employers would find it difficult to accept the reasons I had left work, and that generally, employers favour those candidates who are currently employed. Getting back into my profession was going to be tough, so I had been much better than anyone else in locating the right job prospects and at interviews.

I read many books and spoke to many professionals to educate myself in the art of job search. Eventually, I found a job as a human resources contractor and began to enjoy moving from one assignment to another every six– twelve months. The constant change in work required even greater job search skill, and it was here that I learned the art of job networking as a powerful tool.

However, life is not perfect, and I expect the unexpected from time to time. Eventually, I got married and had two young children and a mortgage. My wife chose to leave her job and stay home to look after our children until they were school age.

This made me the sole income earner for my family, and all the financial responsibility rested with me. So what do you think happened just three months after the birth of our second child?

My boss walked into my office unexpectedly and made my position redundant! The company was restructuring after a takeover, and I was a luxury they could no longer afford – I was part of a cost-cutting exercise and, with many other professionals, I became an unemployment statistic.

I had to register at Centrelink for the first time in my life and apply for government benefits to support my family. So how do you think I felt, one moment I had a respected role in a large company and the next I was lining up at Centrelink to register for benefits?

To make things even more difficult, it had occurred in mid-November when the job market traditionally slows down before Christmas and doesn't pick up again until early February.

It made my search even harder because those few jobs available were hotly contested. It was the sort of stuff that worries you to death, not just for reasons of career and ambition but for the welfare of your loved ones who need you to provide financial support.

So, what do you do, panic and lose confidence? No, I thought it through and developed a plan. How you go about getting your next job is all about planning the job search. It was at this point that I developed the *5 Key Critical Success Factors* to finding a job. It became my job search system.

Let's recap these as follows:

1. Successful job search skills knowledge
2. Strong financial management initiatives
3. Flexible and open career re-assessment
4. Mental toughness and a strong belief system
5. Managing your current job.

Whereas in the past, I had relied upon successful job search skills knowledge and flexible and open career re-assessment, now a new element was introduced into my job search framework. Strong financial management initiatives and mental toughness became important elements for survival.

Firstly, I was the only breadwinner, and I had to keep paying the bills without knowing where my next pay packet would come from.

Secondly, I had to believe in my abilities and be mentally tough to get through this dip in my life. One important thing I learned from this experience was that you could easily fall into a trap called 'learned helplessness'.

That is an ongoing and negative attitude to your current situation that can send you into a downward spiral. I believe this is the reason why some people become long-term unemployed and lose faith in themselves and their abilities. By using the five key critical success factors, I found a job in six weeks and started work in my new role in mid-January.

I learned one vital point that will always be my focus in job search, 'Jobs go to those who are good at getting jobs!'

You must have self-confidence, a strong belief in yourself and a 'never say die' attitude. If you are determined, new job opportunities will present themselves.

ABOUT THE AUTHOR

Anthony Ranieri is Melbourne based with a Bachelor's Degree in Human Resources. He has worked in a variety of permanent and contract management positions in the human resources area and has a thorough knowledge of recruitment, training and development, employee relations, change management and human resource management. Anthony developed his fascination for corporate cultures when he became a professional contractor and was required to "dip into" the job market every six to twelve months. He has seen several organisational cultures at work and reminiscent of the best parts of his experience in this book.

Working in the human resource area helped Anthony to look at the world of work from a different perspective, so he understands corporate politics and the things people will do to get there, even in the satirical sense.

His first book, *How to Find a Job in 6 Weeks* was published in 2003 by Tandem Press in Australia and New Zealand. He has published a second book, *Corporate Psycho —An Expose and Mocumentary on the Adventures of Max Clarke.*

www.ingramcontent.com/pod-product-compliance
Lightning Source LLC
Chambersburg PA
CBHW050505210326
41521CB00011B/2335